Distorted
Development

Series in Political Economy
and Economic Development in Latin America

Series Editor
Andrew Zimbalist
Smith College

Distorted Development: Mexico in the World Economy, David Barkin

State and Capital in Mexico: Development Policy Since 1940, James M. Cypher

Central America: The Future of Economic Integration, edited by George Irvin and Stuart Holland

Struggle Against Dependence: Nontraditional Export Growth in Central America and the Caribbean, edited by Eva Paus

The Peruvian Mining Industry: Growth, Stagnation, and Crisis, Elizabeth Dore

Cuban Political Economy: Controversies in Cubanology, edited by Andrew Zimbalist

†*Rural Women and State Policy: Feminist Perspectives on Latin American Agricultural Development,* edited by Carmen Diana Deere and Magdalena León

The International Monetary Fund and Latin America: Economic Stabilization and Class Conflict, Manuel Pastor, Jr.

†Available in hardcover and paperback.

Distorted Development

Mexico in the World Economy

David Barkin

Westview Press
Boulder • San Francisco • Oxford

Series in Political Economy and Economic Development in Latin America

This Westview softcover edition is printed on acid-free paper and bound in library-quality, coated covers that carry the highest rating of the National Association of State Textbook Administrators, in consultation with the Association of American Publishers and the Book Manufacturers' Institute.

Copyright © 1990 by Westview Press, Inc.

Published in 1990 in the United States of America by Westview Press, Inc., 5500 Central Avenue, Boulder, Colorado 80301, and in the United Kingdom by Westview Press, 36 Lonsdale Road, Summertown, Oxford OX2 7EW

Library of Congress Cataloging-in-Publication Data
Barkin, David.
   Distorted development : Mexico in the world economy / David
Barkin.
      p. cm. — (Series in political economy and economic
development in Latin America)
   Includes bibliographical references and index.
   ISBN 0-8133-7608-4
   1. Mexico—Economic conditions—1982–   . 2. Mexico—Economic
conditions—1970–1982. 3. Mexico—Economic policy—1970–   .
4. Agriculture—Economic aspects—Mexico. 5. Debts, External—
Mexico. 6. Economic stabilization—Mexico. 7. Capital movements—
Mexico. 8. Smuggling—Mexico. I. Title. II. Series.
HC135.B23   1990
330.972′0834—dc20   90-38501
                                                                          CIP

Printed and bound in the United States of America

The paper used in this publication meets the requirements
of the American National Standard for Permanence of Paper
for Printed Library Materials Z39.48-1984.

10   9   8   7   6   5

To
Sol and *Elaine,*
who made a better world

To
Benjamin and *La Raxza;*
the future is yours to change.

Contents

Tables and Figures

Preface

Like most scholarly works, this book is the individualized product of a collective experience. After more than a quarter of a century in Mexico, I have accumulated an enormous debt to colleagues and friends who have unstintingly given of their time, friendship, and insights to assist me in integrating myself into Mexico.

Over the course of these years, the flow of books written abroad into Mexico has turned into a virtual flood, heralding the crisis that finally arrived. Now, fifteen years since the onset of this crisis and in spite of the pious promises of renovated modernists, it appears that the crisis is here to stay, reshaping the country and once again excluding important groups of people who only recently had begun to enjoy some of the benefits of modernization. In observing and participating in the process, I enjoyed a unique opportunity and privileged position in Mexico's pantheon of intellectual luminaries at the very moment when the country reinstated one last burst of nationalistic political fervor.

A few people have been especially important and generous, joining me in the long trek but often choosing different paths, in their commitment to build a better tomorrow. The Universidad Autónoma Metropolitana was created with the promise of a different kind of education. We spent long hours trying to forge a structure that would allow us to realize this promise; I continue to share my dreams and frustrations with colleagues from those heady years, and the results of the collaboration are evident throughout this book: Carlos Rozo, Etelberto Ortiz, and innumerable others have contributed, each in his own fashion, to molding the arguments herein.

When Iván Restrepo invited me to join him at the recently created Centro de Ecodesarrollo I did not dream that this would be the beginning of an enduring collaboration that still offers me the unique opportunity to explore the relationship between the evolving international economy and the local decisions in the most unexpected reaches of Mexico's rural society; in this enterprise, the very special collaborative relationship that I share with Blanca Suárez has permitted us to produce a long series of studies, the results of which have influenced every section of this book.

Gustavo Esteva's quixotic meanderings have not deterred him from championing the need to defend the integrity of people from cultures as diverse as those in his native Oaxaca and of the intellectual gurus from the philosophical world of Ivan Illich; over the years we have struggled in a comradely fashion and frequently managed to develop a common understanding of the fundamental problems oppressing Mexicans. Our joint undertakings have significantly altered both of our lives. Miguel Wionczek, a maverick scholar who always demanded rigor and honesty in our lengthy interchanges, left his indelible mark on my scholarship, in spite of the fact that we never finished writing our joint book. Billie DeWalt returned to Mexico in the early 1980s, taken with the promise of the theory of the internationalization of capital; as in this book, we are continuing to explore the implications of this approach for future developments throughout the Third World.

Even after the book was completed in my mind, however, a long road remained to be traveled. Andy Zimbalist went far beyond the duties of series editor to offer the support and encouragement that helped me to overcome the personal hurdles that popped up throughout the lengthy gestation period. Lucy Conger then stepped in to put her blue pencil to paper while urging me, at my moments of doubt sown by the evolving political scene in Mexico, to get on with the task. Of course, even after finishing the manuscript and sending it off, still other hurdles had to be overcome; in this process, the capable management of the production process by Martha Leggett and the perspicacious editing by Anna Huff transformed the text into a much more readable and consistent product.

Perhaps most telling, my move to Morelia wrought profound transformations. The personal and environmental factors that initiated that process sharpened my understanding of the potential latent in provincial Mexico and the lack of comprehension by official Mexico of this process. This move and the support and challenge offered by Blanca Lemus in the new surroundings made it possible for me to produce the present distillation of Mexico's economic history on the eve of its full integration into the world economy. I hope that the book's promise of a different future is something we will all be able to enjoy.

David Barkin
Morelia, Michoacán

1

Introduction

While thinking about the shape of things to come, I imagined a Mexican leader's nightmare: What if the foreign creditors were magically to write off Mexico's external obligations?

Why a nightmare? Without this external rationale, how could the Mexican government continue to impose the draconian austerity program that has exacted such enormous sacrifices from its people without mass uprisings? What better political scenario could be contrived to justify the thorough restructuring of the Mexican economy presently under way?

For more than a decade Mexico's economy has literally been turned inside out. Traditional strategies have been discarded in favor of new remedies: An open economy with specialization based on comparative advantage is now considered superior to a system that produces for the internal market. Modern technology and international consumption patterns must replace traditional methods and cultures. Dynamic entrepreneurs will break down barriers to economic progress, and people must adapt to the demands of the new productive environment or keep out of its path.

The conventional wisdom holds that the major problem facing Mexico and other Latin American countries is their huge external debt. Yet in analyzing Mexico's problems and in organizing this book, I chose not to do a special chapter on the debt and on the complex negotiations to manage and restructure the country's international financial obligations. Many will criticize this decision. In deciding what to include, I concentrated on the productive transformation of the Mexican economy and the impact it is having on the quality of life for the Mexican people.

This book offers an analysis of some of Mexico's most pressing problems. It is designed to help the reader understand the underlying dynamic processes shaping Mexican society and the Mexican economy. The chapters present a vision of a common pattern of distorted development that assumes unique forms in different parts of economic and social life. Throughout, I try to provide readers with helpful questions that they might bring to the study of other Mexican problems. Although its leaders insist that Mexico is now an urban, industrial country, I am persuaded that effectiveness of the official efforts to transform the country will largely depend, in the ultimate analysis, on the impact such efforts have on rural Mexico. Urban Mexico is incapable of providing productive employment for all of the coming generations of job seekers and certainly cannot handle the pent-up demands of the forgotten cohorts of the past decade. Although only one-third of the population still lives in rural areas, many more still have deep roots there. The rural areas have not only enormous reserves of productive capacity, but also the capability of inducing a sustained process of economic growth.

The new model of outward-looking economic development implanted during the past decade represents a significant shift in priorities. It is based on promoting exports and restructuring domestic industry to achieve international competitiveness. The economic program depends for its success on the continued dynamism of the economies of the advanced industrial countries and on a massive inflow of foreign investment to stimulate export production. But the fundamental underlying assumption of the new development model is the same as that of the old model: The benefits will trickle down to the masses, by employment creation and the spread (linkage) effects of industrialization, through a multiplier that leads to more production. In this new world, resources are no longer supposed to be diverted to protect inefficient domestic industries or small-scale rural producers: If they cannot compete, then they must find some new way to survive.

The new model does not guarantee any place for these displaced producers and their families. It proposes to create an economic environment in which opportunities will exist for those who can seize them. But Mexico is much larger than the four Asian tigers (Hong Kong, Taiwan, Singapore, and South Korea) combined; its population is 85 million and more people still depend on agriculture than industry. In spite of the dramatic growth rates of recent years, the labor-intensive export manufacturing (*maquila*) operations only employ 400,000 people; export production of manufactures does not even occupy as many people as the *maquila*. Even if the international economy were to continue to afford spectacular rates of growth in output in both of these sectors, they cannot respond adequately to the demands of the more than 1 million new entrants into the Mexican labor market during each of the next twenty years.

In this book, then, I question the wisdom of the current approach and offer guidelines for an alternative strategy to economic development. Mexico is sufficiently big and well endowed with natural resources to be able to continue to pursue its present export program while also embarking on a program that would create large numbers of new jobs and forge an internal market in which the vast majority of Mexicans could participate. The underlying thesis, examined in different ways in each of the chapters, is that Mexico's integration into the international market is systematically closing off opportunities, excluding people from participating in the new economy, and polarizing society—offering opportunities for enrichment (licit or not) to a privileged few. Not only does the current system exclude the vast majority from participating in the new economic structures, it also deprives them of the ability to survive by continuing with their traditional activities.

Any viable proposal for change must explicitly take into account this process of international integration and its impact on national society. In previous works, I have stressed the importance of examining this internationalization on a global scale (Barkin 1985; Barkin and Rozo 1981) and in reference to Mexican agriculture (see Chapter 2). With this book I carry the exercise further, pulling together a series of thematic analyses to show how material progress and international integration restructured the Mexican economy in such a way as to impoverish the majority while creating seemingly limitless opportunities for a few. A reckless disregard for the country's natural resources and environment accompanied this process of disenfranchisement. The results are not new or unique; I hope to contribute to an understanding of the tightly interwoven character of national policy making and the demands of international accumulation, as expressed in global markets, financial structures, and relative prices.

The Reorganization of the Mexican Economy

Mexico's transformation is the history of the country's progressive in-tegration into the world economy. In the process the people were wrenched from their local communities and regional cultures into a new national polity and were increasingly subjugated to the designs of an international market. Such economic internationalization is also occurring in most of the other countries of the third world as foreign debt and investment accelerate the reconstruction of social and productive structures. This reorganization of the national economy is enabling countries like Mexico to better supply the affluent industrialized countries with less expensive goods and services. These products facilitate the task of controlling domestic inflation in the richer countries, as well as raising living standards there.

The productive reorganization of Mexico is the focus of this book. Because the reorganization occurred much earlier and more thoroughly in agriculture than anywhere else, I start my analysis with the profound changes occurring in that sector. But the Mexican government, like its counterparts in most of the rest of the world, is convinced that the country's future lies in industrial reorientation to meet the demands of the international economy, even though for years political and social philosophy in Mexico argued just the reverse: Mexico could best develop by responding to the needs of its people as they became more fully integrated into a thriving domestic market. For reasons discussed in Chapter 5, the local market never achieved this dynamism and development was never able to forge an integrated national labor market that offered suitable employment opportunities for all.

In view of this past failure, the prevailing official analysis has now shifted to the opposite extreme. Senior policy makers are now promoting export production and improving Mexico's international competitiveness by reducing real wages and stimulating competition among firms in Mexico and with imports to try to restrain domestic inflation and to limit future devaluations of the peso. In their search for international competitiveness, they have garnered solid support from the leaders of the multilateral financial community and in the governments of Mexico's leading trading partners in the industrial world. This support, however, has not been accompanied by significant concessions from the United States or other trading partners, in the form of easing restrictions on Mexican exports. Mexican policy makers are convinced that this internal liberalization is the only sound basis for future growth. These policy makers are celebrated in the international halls of power; "more papist than the pope" is the best description of their whole-hearted adoption of the neoliberal orthodoxy of the free market economy.

This reorganization is not going unopposed. But the nature of the opposition is harder to discern in Mexico than elsewhere. The profound struggle for survival of urban and rural workers severely limits their ability to develop a viable political alternative. Furthermore, the ever-present threat of military force is a persuasive damper on dissent. In spite of this, the hotly contested 1988 presidential elections and the numerous regional sequels offer testimony to the breadth and depth of the pent-up resentment against the existing system. Unfortunately, the organized opposition offers no real alternative to the official reorganization. At this writing (late 1989), it seems likely that the gradual opening of the existing political system will continue in response to this opposition and to the profound contradictions of past developments. However, it appears unlikely that this democratization will seriously jeopardize the present hegemony of the ruling party, the PRI (*Partido Revolucionario Institucional*, or Party of the Institutional Revolution), or the economic strategy the PRI champions.

Mexico's Relationship with the United States

Other structures in Mexican society sharply curb the need for and possibility of violent dissent. Perhaps the two most important features limiting popular discontent originate in the unique set of bilateral relations the country maintains with the United States. On the one hand, millions of Mexicans depend on their jobs in the north for a substantial part of their income, the sustenance of their families, and even their ability to work in Mexico. Surprisingly, in the wake of the Immigration Reform and Control Act of 1986,[1] many Mexicans claim it is now easier to cross the border and obtain work. This is partly because of the widespread distribution of legalized working papers under the amnesty and the replacement labor recruitment programs;[2] but others report that it is still easy to obtain employment as an undocumented worker in the rural labor market in the United States and that it is now less costly and less dangerous to cross the border than in the past. Remittances by laborers in the United States have become a significant source of foreign exchange for Mexico and are essential for many families, especially in rural Mexico, for basic living expenses and to pay the costs of sowing their subsistence crops.

The second element, less widely commented upon, is the impact of the international food support programs of the U.S. government on Mexican economic policy. As grains still play an important role in the U.S. export picture, its international credit operations encourage and facilitate the Mexican government's decision to abandon its support for small-scale rainfed agriculture. Mexico is able to maintain its cheap food policy by importing growing volumes of foodstuffs—grains, oilseeds, milk, meat—as well as animal feed. Mexico benefits from international competition and from the political demands of farmers in the United States and the European Common Market that have forced the respective governments to spend more than $200 billion (in 1989) on subsidies for food exports. The concessional credit terms of organizations like the U.S. Commodity Credit Corporation further sweeten the pot. Since Mexico purchases the agricultural products on credit, which is simply added to the country's long-term international debt, these imports are seen as effectively free by the present Mexican political leadership, which does not have to concern itself with repaying these long-term obligations. The "soft" export credits require no budgetary outlays during the present six-year presidential term; in fact, the public sale of this imported food represents net income to the government.

Other elements in this bilateral relationship also influence the changing shape of the Mexican economy. Foreign investment is virtually flooding into the country in response to the new outward orientation of the Mexican authorities and their "clarification" of Mexican investment laws, which now permit full foreign ownership of plants in most relevant industries. Tourism, too, is increasing in response to greater investment by international firms and eased restrictions about the repatriation of profits. Finally, in spite of increased prosecution in the war against drug trafficking, the sustained vitality of the U.S. demand for drugs offers a continuing temptation to poverty-afflicted farmers who see marijuana cultivation as an easy way to counteract the discriminatory policies of the Mexican government against basic food production. (Scant importance is attached to the possibility that the export subsidies may dry up as a result of an agreement between the United States and the European Economic Community or that exogenous global trends—growing demand and declining production as a result of worldwide ecological changes— may restrict the volume of grains available on international markets while also raising grain prices.)

The Debt Crisis and a New Era in International Relations

Mexico's international debt is now second only to Brazil's among third world nations. The erudite and loudly contested debates about what the resources were used for or who appropriated them are themes of the past. The threats of reprisals against the *sacadólares*, or agents of capital flight, have waned as the wave of reprivatization of the economy grows to encompass even the heretofore sacrosanct petroleum and telecommunications industries. As the petroleum boom evaporated and interest rates rose, interest and amortization payments on the foreign debt became so burdensome as to force Mexico to the brink of declaring a moratorium in 1982; the Mexican crisis ushered in a new epoch in international economic relations, for the international financial community finally recognized that the problem was not limited to Mexico.

Time and again since that momentous period, Mexico has returned to the negotiating table. In each successive round, it has demonstrated itself to be a responsible member of the international community, fulfilling its obligations to the letter and often beyond the spirit of the agreement. Mexico has been rewarded with increasingly generous terms for restructuring the debt and capitalizing interest payments and, most recently, with a slight reduction of its real burden. But these agreements only postpone the day of reckoning; meanwhile the burden of servicing the international debt continues to exact its toll. As if this were not enough, now the internal debt, owed to the very rich in Mexico, costs even more to service than the foreign debt because interest rates have been kept high to attract capital to finance the persisting budget deficits.

The issue of the foreign debt should not be analyzed as simply a repayment problem. Tomes have been written on the debt problem and Mexico's place in the global picture from this perspective. Mexico, like most other third world countries, can never be expected to pay off its debt. Rather, the debt and the crisis that it sparked have already done their service in the international economy: They have forced a reorganization of production and of social classes that places the affected countries in a much better position to attend to the demands of the wealthy in the rich countries, as the dramatic decline in the prices of such countries' raw materials, manufactured products, and labor lowers costs and raises profits. In addition, countries like Mexico now openly court international capital so that they may participate in the process; as a result, the profits are also concentrated in the coffers of the world's economic power centers.

The repeated renegotiations of terms that have occupied an important part of the time of Mexico's leading policy makers will continue. There are bookkeeping problems to resolve and demands for the political victories that such theatrical "happenings" offer. But the main impact of the debt, and of the economic crisis that it reflects, has been to usher in new regimes in the most important economies of the third world. In Mexico, the neoliberal economic teams are flinging open the floodgates of international competition and foreign investment. They have little patience for the shrill cries from small or even large local businesses that are folding under the onslaught; poor farmers—or members of the informal sector, as the marginal are now politely classified—have even less of a chance for a hearing.

It is no wonder that this is a time for celebration and optimism in the arena of international economic relations. The conditions are ripe for increasing economic cooperation, or for the penetration of the international economy, depending on the perspective of the speaker. The optimism spreading in the international press reflects the new opportunities Mexico offers to the international business community: the contribution it promises to continue to make to international accumulation. It is small wonder that the new (1989) government in Mexico is basking in the warmth of international acclaim. A doubt remains, however: If, as is likely, the new inflow of foreign capital and loans does not generate large numbers of new jobs or permit an easing of restrictions on social programs, will the regime continue to be able to invent new tricks to calm the people?

A Comment on Method

This book was written in Mexico by an academic trained in the United States. Its structure and the organization of the evidence to support the underlying arguments are a reflection of this uncomfortable meeting of two different worlds. It does not meet the standards of either: The positivistic tests of the U.S. academe are patently absent as are the philosophical discourse and assumptions of Mexican political economy. Rather, the book is a peculiar blend of currents from both societies. The world has never evolved as the lineal projection of past trends, and yet past victories and errors continually define the limits for changes that can be wrought by waves of human beings struggling to survive and improve their lot.

Thus, this book envelopes an approach to social analysis and change. By mustering a modicum of evidence and leaning on the heterogeneous accumulation of literature from both sides of the border that describes the Mexican experience, I hope to persuade readers of the seriousness, if not the validity, of the analysis while not leaving them stranded without an idea of the implications of this critique. As a North American living in Mexico, precluded from direct participation in the political process but directly concerned about its outcome, it would be unrealistic for me to pretend that I remain aloof from the intense political struggles of the era.

The book evolved from my professional practice as an economist and my personal understanding of change, abstractly and in very concrete circumstances. It begins with an analysis of the disastrous reverses of Mexico's glorious and bloody agricultural history. It does not begin there because rural production is the largest part of the Mexican economy today (it is not), but rather because rural production is the point of departure for present development. The massive distribution of land created the basis for achieving food self-sufficiency while the rural sector financed the country's early industrialization. The revolutionary heritage even paved the way for the successful modernization of a small part of rural Mexico, which has become a prosperous showcase of capitalist organization. Today, the powerful elite that dominates the rural export and livestock sectors has joined with the national leaders to prevent the large majority of Mexican farmers from escaping poverty or contributing to the country's next stage of economic growth.

The book also ends with a return to agriculture. After years of study and reflection on the achievements of industrialization, of the spread of the comforts of the modern world, it seems clearer than ever that the urban, industrial model of social and economic organization is incapable of providing adequate answers to the aspirations of the vast majority of people in the third world. In the last chapter I build upon the dismal heritage of "stabilizing development" and more recent development programs to suggest that a revival of small-scale food production in Mexico's central plateau offers the most viable basis for resuscitating the Mexican economy as a whole and for reinjecting vigor into Mexico's extraordinary society.

It seems appropriate to anticipate some of the criticisms of this approach. This is not a plea to protect the "noble savage" or to recreate the cooperative indigenous farming villages of yore. Rather, the argument stems from the recognition that present development policies will be unable to incorporate the millions of people in rural areas into the productive folds. Rather than toss them off as flotsam, rejecting their humanity and destroying them as the residue of industrial progress, I suggest that they can survive, maybe even flourish, in a world organized by themselves in symbiosis with modernity. At best, existing policies condemn these sizable groups to marginality; at worst, to misery and extinction. But people do not normally accept their damnation passively. The small farmers as a group are too important an actor in Mexico's history for politicians to simply write them off without considering their reactions and exploring the alternative presented at the end of this book.

The intervening chapters contain the history of recent blunders. Mexico, one of seven countries of "megabiodiversity" in the world (along with Australia, Brazil, Colombia, Indonesia, Madagascar, and Zaire), is suffering an environmental crisis that extends far beyond the horrors of what is reputedly the most contaminated city in the world. Perhaps even more distressing than the decades of abuse and neglect is the bleak perspective facing the country as it proceeds to implement orthodox solution schemes ever more broadly. Industrialization is supplying the beneficiaries of distorted development with the goods, but neither the producers nor the consumers have found a way to effectively confront the horrors industrialization is creating.

In the third chapter I examine the particular forms this disaster is taking in Mexico. The beneficiaries of Mexican development have shown themselves quite able to appropriate a disproportionate share of the spoils. Although this has been amply documented to some degree in virtually all tracts on the Mexican economic experience, much emphasis has been placed on the role of corruption. I take a different approach in the fourth chapter, tracing the process by which producers can extract an extra measure of profit from the system at the very moments when the country is in most need. The liberal economist might respond that this is a result of inappropriate policies, but my analysis suggests that if "prices were right," capital flight would have proceeded in less devious ways because of the fundamental underlying disagreement between workers, farmers, and capitalists about how to divide the national income.

Industrialization and stabilization policies, the subjects of chapters 5 and 6, are tributes to a cynical view of a nation's relationship to its populace. The "Mexican miracle" that successfully incorporated millions into the folds of modernization disintegrated into the morass of debt-fueled crisis. After wresting peasants from their traditional forms of social organization and production, the new Mexican society was unable to offer them productive jobs; instead they were encouraged to congregate in the overcrowded slums or migrate to the United States. When the bubble burst, they could not be sent back home, nor could they continue to be supplied with public services. To make Mexico competitive, the former peasants were being thrust into the corners of Mexican society— marginalized, as the Mexicans express it—but the constant question is: For how long?

This book addresses these issues. Rather than just providing answers, I have attempted to fortify readers with questions that they can bring to the rest of the literature. In today's world of international development pundits, we would make a great stride forward by recognizing that at least part of the solution must come from allowing the majority of people not actually incorporated into the modern world to eke out a living on their own terms rather than subjugating them to a system that finds even their oppression too expensive.

Notes

1. The Immigration Reform and Control Act of 1986 was designed to control the flow of workers to the United States and regularize the status of many illegal immigrants already in the United States by declaring an amnesty for people who could document their regular presence and employment in the country during the previous three years; after the amnesty period, during which more than 1.5 million people applied to be recognized as legal aliens, the government threatened to become much stricter with employers hiring people without legal immigration papers.

2. The Seasonal Agricultural Worker (SAW) and Replacement Agricultural Worker programs were designed to allow a substantial number of migratory workers to obtain working papers to come to the United States for jobs in rural areas. Another 1 million workers have applied for papers under the SAW program.

2

The End to Food Self-sufficiency

In this chapter I reveal how the process of internationalization heightened Mexico's problems of rural underdevelopment. After having achieved food self-sufficiency and raised rural living standards in the thirty years leading up to the mid-1960s, the country is now plagued by a profound agricultural crisis. It has ceased to be self-sufficient in food.[1] No longer are its tortillas made from locally grown raw materials; nor does it supply all of its demand for meat and dairy products or even animal feed. This crisis has its origins in economic policies of the 1960s and was exacerbated by a great drought in 1979–1980. In 1981, the Aztec rain god Tlaloc cooperated; together with a government food program (the Mexican Food System or SAM), initiated by the president to lead the country back to the road of food self-sufficiency, the end of the drought brought a dramatic but temporary increase in agricultural production and an improvement in nutritional standards. But money and rain were not enough to overcome the obstacles that created the crisis in agriculture, which persists in spite of and amidst high agricultural growth rates. Although the phenomenon is apparently contradictory, the crisis is the result of a successful agricultural growth strategy that reoriented production toward agro-exports and animal feeds. This strategy has created serious natural resource disequilibria, un- and underemployment, inadequate food production, and impoverishment.

These same trends are being repeated in many developing countries today (Barr 1981; DeWalt 1983; Paulino and Mellor 1984; Barkin, Batt, and DeWalt 1990). Agricultural modernization is destroying old forms of social and economic organization in many parts of the world. This is nothing new: History contains many stories of dramatic shifts in productive, social, and economic structures as a result of the expanding capitalist system (Wolf 1982). What is new is the rhythm with which

---

This chapter incorporates substantial parts of an article titled "Sorghum and the Mexican Food Crisis," written jointly with Billie R. DeWalt and published in the Fall 1988 issue (Vol. 20:3, pp. 30–59) of the *Latin American Research Review*. Used by permission.

the phenomenon is occurring today and the similarity of these transformations throughout the world. With the international dissemination
of new technology, new forms of organization of production, mass
marketing techniques, and the spread of new items of consumption,
increasingly homogeneous (national) systems are created; in the process,
cultural idiosyncracies are modified.

The Internationalization of Mexican Agriculture

Agricultural development proceeds through a complex interaction of
market pressures and government policy. Through the price system, the
market guides producers toward the most profitable crops. National
economic policy rearranges market priorities by modifying prices and
profit rates in different activities; historically, governments have accorded
priority to industrialization and export. In Mexico (as elsewhere), this
bias precipitated the present problem of food dependency.

Mexican agriculture has been strongly influenced by the rapid transformation of the whole society. Neither investors nor government have
displayed any concern for the destruction of traditional social structures
and industries. In fact, policy makers often rejoice at how rapidly
agriculture has overcome its traditional heritage. Growth takes place in
a permissive atmosphere in which government policy creates the favorable
conditions that permit the market to mandate the most profitable sectors.
In this environment, basic foods producers are at a decided disadvantage
as technology and politics combine with market forces to privilege
commercial farmers.

The most apparent force determining agricultural production is the
price system in national markets. In Mexico, as in many other countries,
however, international prices strongly influence local prices. Even when
there is substantial state intervention, international grain prices exert a
powerful influence in policy decisions about the level and direction of
change of local prices.[2] International prices, like national prices for grains
and other commodities, are themselves shaped by powerful groups: The
world grain trade is tightly controlled by seven large corporations (Morgan
1979), while political and economic struggles within and competition
among the major grain-producing countries also affect prices.

These global market determinants have become firmly rooted in the
Mexican economic system. Of course, national differences—resources
and history—intervene to put their own distinctive imprint on the
process, but in the realm of economics, national boundaries have ceased
to be barriers. For some time, the Mexican leadership has promoted the
integration of Mexico into the world market as a national priority. Leaders

have stimulated this assimilation process and imposed the global (rather than a national) system of priorities on the country. These global priorities now influence the allocation of resources and the formulation of policy.

In this reordering, the state is continually perfecting its ability to intervene. While generally accepting the guidelines of the global market, it modifies them by changing the relative prices of some goods or altering priorities when this seems appropriate or necessary. The need for such modifications may arise with the increase in popular discontent among workers or farmers or for strategic reasons related to other internal problems. The Mexican Food System (SAM) was one striking response to the social problems of poverty and unrest in rural Mexico and the foreign exchange burden of massive food imports.[3] Exceptional programs such as this one, and other measures that benefit the majority directly, brake the pace of economic growth. As a result, governments undertake such programs only in response to strong and effective political pressures, which oblige the state to seek constructive responses that partially compensate for the heavy social costs of existing growth strategies, such as the exacerbation of social and economic inequalities.[4]

The incorporation of new countries and regions into industrial production and the growth of the labor force are characteristics of the internationalization of capital. From this process, a new international division of labor (NIDL) emerges involving a new (for Latin America) export orientation and the massive incorporation of people into the wage-labor force.[5] As their isolation and independence erode, these groups of people become building blocks in a system in which self-sufficiency appears to be anathema. Producing goods for the mere survival of low-wage workers is not as profitable as producing for more affluent markets. Thus, as people come to depend on production by others, they become more vulnerable: Unless it is profitable to sell to the workers, the goods will not be produced. A contradiction arises because the swelling unemployment in most third world countries allows employers to pay low wages, making it difficult for workers to become consumers. Thus, the internationalization of capital and the NIDL work at odds with policies to assure food self-sufficiency (Barkin and Rozo 1981) in a world where unemployment and poorly paid workers coexist with profit maximizers (Barkin and Suárez 1985).

This explanation of the emergence of a new crisis in Mexican agriculture is based on the theory of the internationalization of capital. The better known dependency approach assigns blame to the exploitative relationships promulgated by developed countries or transnational corporations (e.g., Rama and Vigorito 1979; Garreau 1980; Chilcote 1982; Vigorito 1984). There is a growing recognition that dependency theory is overly simplistic and inadequate as an explanation (Cardoso 1977; Jenkins 1984) and that most forms of dependency theory have two principal weaknesses. One is the theory's assumption that everything dynamic flows from the core to the periphery. As Carol Smith (1980), Billie DeWalt (1985a), and others are demonstrating, individuals and institutions in the third world are increasingly asserting themselves with greater efficacy in the face of attempts by the core countries to impose their will in the third world. A second weakness is that the historical methods so prevalent in dependency theory lead to an inability to account for the dynamics of the current situation; it is almost as though history happened "once upon a time" and no longer exerts any influence.

In Mexico, the internationalization of capital (Palloix 1975; Rozo and Barkin 1983; Jenkins 1984) is reorganizing local, regional, national, and international systems of production, distribution, and consumption to facilitate the process of capital accumulation. As the global economic system penetrates even the most isolated corners of each country, small producers are wrested from their subsistence economy and thrust into a different world, one of wage earners and job seekers. But this new world is incapable of supplying sufficient opportunities to fulfill the hopes and implied promises of its far-reaching claims: Employment possibilities are limited and welfare programs are virtually nonexistent. As long as the market structures in the more affluent countries determine what and how materials are produced in the poorer regions, it will be virtually impossible for the latter to reorient their economies to provide for the needs of the majority of their populations.

Reformers clamoring for a new international order are not the only ones who see the world in this light. People of many persuasions bemoan the loss of national self-sufficiency to the modernizing forces that extend and deepen patterns of dependency. A U.S. diplomat, analyzing a violent outbreak in Micronesia (a colonial territory in the Pacific), commented:

> If we examine our effects on the island culture, we see they have a real case. Before the U.S. arrived, the natives were self-sufficient, they picked their food off the trees or fished. Now, since we have them hooked on consumer goods, they'd starve without a can opener. Some of the radical independence leaders want to reverse this and develop the old self-sufficiency. We can't blame them. However, we can't leave. We need our military bases there. We have no choice. As some of my friends in Washington say, you've got to grab them by the balls, their minds and hearts will follow (Maccoby 1976:18).

The end to food self-sufficiency, therefore, is a normal part of the expansion of the market. The theory of the internationalization of capital explains why: The move from basic food production to more profitable crops is the only way to expand the base from which to extract profit. It is one part of a broader process that increases profits and assures the balanced production of goods needed for social and economic stability. But since it also fosters the disorganization of communities, it augurs the onset of political unrest because of the inability of many nations to create the economic and social opportunities required to productively absorb displaced groups into new activities.

Producers at all levels—in the present case, Mexican small farmers, large farmers, food processors, and transnational corporations—find it in their best interests to move toward the most modern and productive methods of cultivation, management, and marketing, to turn out profitable commodities. With the dissemination of information about world market prices, the search for efficient and profitable lines of production has led to the accelerated diffusion and adoption of technological innovations. On the demand side, rising incomes among certain social groups and changing worldwide consumption patterns are pushing farmers toward new products. These processes are indicators of the internationalization of capital, which is integrating individual producers into the emerging world system. In the rest of this chapter I explore the problems that arise as this assimilation proceeds. This exploration is divided into four parts.

1. A brief discussion of Mexican agricultural history since 1940 reveals impressive growth and profound changes. These data demonstrate both Mexico's "agricultural miracle" as well as its increasing food supply problems.

2. A review of the spectacular growth of sorghum[6] cultivation in Mexico—a technological success story termed Mexico's second Green Revolution (DeWalt 1985b)—reveals its part in the processes of modernization and continuing underdevelopment. In terms of crop adoption and increase in hectares sown, sorghum has been an even greater success than wheat, the first Green Revolution crop (Hewitt de Alcántara 1976).

3. The changes that are a central part of the process of Mexico's integration into the world economy are discussed. Such changes are being driven both by world market trends as well as by demand forces and investment decisions occurring within countries like Mexico. Mexican government policies have followed and been guided by the model of comparative advantage (Barkin, Batt, and DeWalt, 1990:107–110), which led to the present difficulties. These processes precipitated an agricultural and food crisis—indicated by the necessity for importing huge quantities of basic foodstuffs, by the balance of agricultural trade becoming negative, by the continuing undernourishment of a large and growing proportion of the population, and by the increasing underutilization of land and labor in rural Mexico.

4. Any suggestion for an alternative strategy to confront the crisis must explicitly take into account the distortions caused by using the model of comparative advantage. This chapter concludes with the suggestion that a strategy of food self-sufficiency in Mexico would not only be efficient but would also contribute to reversing the profound economic and social crises in which the country presently finds itself. In the process, this strategy would also improve the balance of payments and reduce the government deficit.

Transformation of the Agricultural Sector in Mexico

The transformation of Mexican agriculture is amply documented (e.g., Barkin 1981–1982; CESPA 1982; Rama and Rello 1982; Barkin and Suárez 1985).[7] This section synthesizes the most important of the factors guiding this change and traces their impacts on rural Mexico. The two most important phenomena to influence the evolution of land utilization patterns in Mexico are the notable increase in the area cultivated and the marked change in the composition of crops grown.

The Growth and Intensified Use of Cultivated Area

Small producers thrived in the decades following the Mexican Revolution. The resulting redistribution of lands and formation of *ejido* communities[8] opened the possibility of more systematic and intensive cultivation of regions previously abandoned or underutilized by large landowners. Even though a large part of the *ejidal* grants consisted of marginal lands, the agrarian reform provided small producers with the freedom to produce basic commodities for family and local community consumption. Together with small improvements in the quality and quantity of inputs (e.g., fertilizers and plaguicides), credit, and technical assistance for basic grain production, increased participation of smallholders contributed to achieving national self-sufficiency in the production of maize by the end of the 1950s. Some years later, the contradictions emerging from the redistribution of lands reappeared as a barrier to the dynamism of the *ejidal* sector.

Public investment in irrigation facilities also contributed to the growth in cultivated area. Between 1940 and 1979, irrigation works, primarily in large districts, accounted for from 70 percent to 99.2 percent of government investment in the agricultural sector (Barkin and King 1970; S. Walsh 1984:118). The resources were concentrated principally in the three key northern states of Sonora, Sinaloa, and Tamaulipas (Barkin and Suárez 1985:Table 10). Mexico's irrigated area now amounts to almost one-third of its cultivated area (Table 2.1), the highest proportion of irrigated to total cultivated land out of all countries in temperate and tropical zones.

Since 1940, cultivated area has expanded at a rate of more than 2.4 percent annually. The area cultivated increased more than 2.5 times while the area opened to irrigation increased even more rapidly, to more than 3 times the area of 1940 (Table 2.1). These figures account for the substantial increase in agricultural production during the period and resulted in a growth in cumulative annual employment in modern agriculture of 2.3 percent between 1950 and 1980. In contrast, the growth of agricultural employment in the rest of Latin America was barely 0.5 percent (Couriel 1984:55).

Change in Crop Composition

Significant changes in national and international markets and the internationalization of agriculture also occasioned changes in land utilization, with a tendency toward more intensive use of available resources and a search for more profitable crops. At first, most policy makers joined with the farmers in emphasizing the production of food for the Mexican population. Both groups were content to increase output of staple crops as a way of improving producer profits and supplying domestic markets. The agrarian reform and the construction of irrigation works were originally defended by policy makers as means to solve the problem of feeding the population. The agricultural sector was also generating sizable amounts of foreign exchange from traditional agro-exports to fund industrialization.

Large landholders led the change. Many were obliged by economic pressures and the threat of further land expropriation to stop treating their land simply as an element of status or prestige, as they had often done previously; politics reinforced market forces to stimulate a more intensive pattern of cultivation directly oriented toward the production of profit. Traditional basic foodgrain production became less profitable as small farmers began to cultivate their new plots and urban and industrial groups pressured for price controls on grains.

As a consequence, a new group of commercial farmers made major changes in technology, abandoning the traditional use of land in favor of more capital-intensive exploitation using fertilizers, pesticides, improved seeds, mechanization, and other practices to increase productivity and profitability.[9] For example, at the end of the 1970s the use of fertilizers was growing at an annual rate of about 13 percent, and between 1940 and 1980 the number of tractors in the country grew at a rate of over 9 percent per year (DGEA 1983:27). The increasing availability of

TABLE 2.1
Basic Indicators of Rural Development

	1940	1960	1980	1989[a]	Annual Rates of Growth		
					1940-1960	1960-1980	1980-1989
Population[b]	19,654	36,046	66,847	84,278	3.1	3.1	2.6
Harvested Area[c]							
Maize	5,900	11,364	16,966	16,857	3.3	2.0	−0.1
Beans	3,340	5,558	6,766	6,175	2.6	1.0	−1.0
Wheat	631	840	1,551	1,293	1.4	3.1	−2.0
Rice	602	1,326	724	1,135	4.0	−3.0	5.1
Soybeans	0	4	154	480		20.0	13.5
Sorghum	0	116	1,543	1,545		13.8	0
Irrigated Area[c]	1,732	3,408	4,898	5,391	3.4	1.8	1.1
Animal Production[d]							
Beef		610	1,031	625		6.8	−5.4
Pork		573	1,251	714		4.0	−6.0
Chicken		194	399	531		3.7	3.2
Eggs		401	866	815		3.9	−0.7
Milk		4,915	6,742	5,076		1.6	−3.1

[a]Estimated.
[b]Thousands of people.
[c]Areas are in thousands of hectares.
[d]Series begin in 1972. Thousands of tons for meat and eggs; millions of liters for milk.

Sources: SARH (Secretaría de Agricultura y Recursos Hidráulicos), *Estadísticas Básicas 1960-1986 para la Planeación del Desarrollo Rural Integral,* Mexico City: SARH, 1986; SARH, *Econotecnica Agrícola,* "Consumos Aparentes de Productos Agrícolas, 1925–1982," Vol. 7:9, Sept. 1983; Carlos Salinas de Gortari, *Primer Informe de Gobierno 1989,* Mexico City: Poder Ejecutivo Federal, 1989, Anexo.

government agricultural credit for wealthy farmers lowered the cost of these and other inputs and facilitated the expansion of the physical productivity of the land; in fact, the credit to the rich probably came at the expense of financing to the poorer farmers.[10] Under these conditions, there would have been an increase in the volume and value of agricultural production even without a substantial increase in the area under cultivation. The trend toward capital-intensive exploitation had three important effects: (1) permanent agricultural jobs were replaced by machinery; (2) employees and migratory labor were substituted for independent workers; and (3) the ability of agriculture to continue absorbing new workers was reduced. These tremendous social and economic dislocations are evident in the statistics. While the share of people working in agriculture declined, hired labor in the rural modern sector expanded from 31.7 percent of the total work force in agriculture in 1950 to 51 percent in 1980. But there was an *absolute reduction* in the number of self-employed agricultural workers (Couriel 1984:56).

This modernization of Mexican agriculture since 1965 has been characterized by a phenomenal growth of the livestock sector. The data in Table 2.1 show that the production of pigs, chickens, and cattle grew rapidly until the onset of the crisis in the 1980s. Per capita consumption of eggs doubled in the last forty years, poultry production increased sixfold in the past thirty years to about 350 million birds, and hog production grew almost as rapidly to about 10 million head in 1990 (Table 2.1; Salinas de Gortari 1989:86–87). This expansion was accompanied by an industrial transformation that led to the animals being enclosed in buildings and tended to in factory-like conditions instead of the back yards of a previous era.

Natural pastures, household wastes, agricultural residues, and other similar resources once used for household production of livestock were replaced by technological systems that now rely on cultivated pastures, improved breeds of animals, heavy use of antibiotics, and confined feeding of industrially produced, balanced animal feeds; this process advanced at an extraordinary pace among poultry producers and has since encompassed significant parts of the hog and dairy sectors (Suárez and Barkin 1990). As a result, land utilization has been changing rapidly to respond to the better-paying demand for green fodder, feed grains, and oilseeds. The technology used for cattle, pig, and poultry production now depends on animal feeds that are produced from basic grains and the residues (oilseed cakes) that remain once vegetable oils are extracted from oilseeds, thereby creating competition between livestock and humans for the use of the country's land and other agricultural resources.[11] The data in Table 2.1 show clearly the displacement of basic grains (maize, wheat, rice, and beans)[12] by soybeans, alfalfa, sorghum, oats, and other products intimately related to modern agricultural and livestock production. The diversified *milpa* (maize complex) with its subsidiary production of beans, squash, and other crops, as well as the fodder and other inputs for the household economy, relinquished its hold on the country's best lands as specialized production systems spread inexorably; in the process the social basis for the small family farm was seriously compromised.

Specialization in use of agricultural land in the country is more complex than just a simple expansion toward livestock products. Also notable is an important growth in the area cultivated with fruits and vegetables, a process stimulated by agro-industrial investment (Feder 1977; Rama and Vigorito 1979). At the same time, in certain parts of government, there was a greater concern for the profitable commercial production of crops like cotton, coffee, and tobacco. Expansion in some other important commodities has been stimulated almost exclusively by private initiative reacting to market signals and incentives. Such is the case with the production of chickpeas for export and of grapes as a raw material for national agro-industrial production.

This specialization and intensification reduced the share of basic food crops in national production as other products proved more profitable. Government policy and the greater influence of world market prices on producer decisions greatly accelerated these changes. The land area planted in the four basic foods declined from three-quarters of the total at the beginning of the 1940s to less than half by 1980. The land dedicated to maize, wheat, and beans has been generally declining since 1965 (Figure 2.1). These three basic food crops went from being cultivated on almost 11 million hectares to less than 9 million in thirty years, while the total land under cultivation increased by almost 50 percent. Rising yields were insufficient to keep up with population growth and increasing per capita consumption during the years of economic growth. This displacement of basic grains for direct human consumption has required the importation of enormous quantities of food to meet the needs of the urban and, increasingly, the rural population. Between 1980 and 1985 maize imports accounted for as much as one-quarter of national consumption, rising as high as 35 percent in 1980 and 1983 (Barkin and Suárez 1985:Table 19); the problem of high volumes of food imports still plagues the country in 1990. Consumer complaints about tortillas made from imported yellow maize (used as animal feed in the United States) reflect the resulting deterioration of the nutritional and cosmetic quality of this important part of the Mexican diet.

Despite the insufficient production of basic grains in the country, large areas of rainfed lands have been abandoned. The government estimates more than 10 million hectares of arable land were idle during

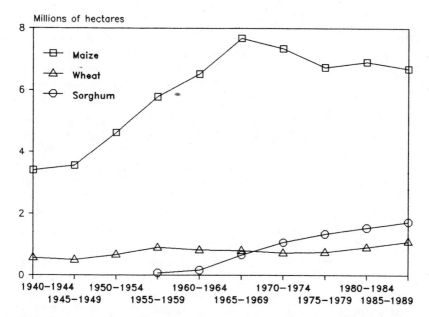

FIGURE 2.1   Harvested Area of Maize, Wheat, and Sorghum, 1940–1989

Sources: SARH (Secretaría de Agricultura y Recursos Hidráulicos), *Estadísticas Básicas 1960–1986 para la Planeación del Desarrollo Rural Integral*, Mexico City: SARH, 1986; SARH, *Econotecnica Agrícola*, "Consumos Aparentes de Productos Agrícolas, 1925–1982," Vol. 7:9, Sept. 1983; Carlos Salinas de Gortari, *Primer Informe de Gobierno 1989*, Mexico City: Poder Ejecutivo Federal, 1989, Anexo.

the 1988 summer crop cycle.[13] This wholesale abandonment of cultivation of potentially productive rainfed lands is the result of policies to restrict price increases for basic food grains, which predominate in rainfed agriculture, and the unwillingness to provide the necessary credit and inputs for the productive exploitation of these areas. Recently, even as the government reasserted its commitment to food self-sufficiency, officially fixed producer prices continued to evolve unfavorably against food production, having declined to less than 70 percent of the already depressed levels of 1980 by the end of 1988. As might be predicted, production declined as profit margins were squeezed and became negative. Agriculture was not even able to export enough to pay for the basic grains and other needed food imports during the first half of the 1980s, at a time when national economic policy was promoting exports in all sectors.[14]

To summarize, Mexican agriculture has shown great dynamism. In both quantitative as well as qualitative terms, a rapid rhythm of change is evident. This dynamism reflects in large part the emergence of a group of entrepreneurial farmers who base productive decisions on the profitability of alternative crops. It also reflects the success of government policies to promote agricultural and livestock development in response to priorities determined by market demand by the richest 30 percent of the population rather than by the needs of the majority of the Mexican population. The growing agricultural area in use and the intensification of cultivation have *not* been dedicated to the production of basic grains for human consumption. Instead, the new agricultural lands have been devoted to the production of export and animal crops.

The displacement of basic grain production has become even more pronounced in recent years, once the physical expansion of land has slowed. Because of this, *the transformation of Mexican agriculture must be seen as not just a change in the type of products offered but also as changes in the way productive decisions are made and in how and for whom commodities are produced.* The dynamics of Mexican agriculture have led to the abandonment of rainfed lands by small farmers as production has become unprofitable. Research into basic food production in rainfed areas has also been deficient, thus depriving smallholders of the kinds of technological innovations that others have taken advantage of to spur commercial production. Furthermore, small farmers have not received the technical and material support required either to increase the productivity of their basic food production or to reorient their production toward more remunerative commercial crops. While the *Sistema Alimentario Mexicano (SAM)*, the country's much-vaunted drive for food self-sufficiency launched in 1980, briefly slowed these trends, there has been a reversion to the original patterns following the dismantling of the SAM in 1982 (see Austin and Esteva 1987:Introduction and Barkin 1987). Subsequent declarations of intentions to achieve food self-sufficiency have not been supported by changes in the system of relative prices or by government assistance to translate the rhetoric into reality (Barkin and Suárez 1985).

The History of Sorghum in Mexico

To illustrate some of these trends it is useful to consider the expansion of sorghum cultivation and use. Sorghum is a grain native to Africa that is used exclusively as an animal feed in the United States and

Mexico; it was unknown in the traditional agriculture of Mexico. Except for a few exceptional, unsuccessful experiments during the first half of the century, it was not cultivated systematically. In 1944, however, foreign agronomists from the recently created Office of Special Studies—established through an agreement between the Rockefeller Foundation and Mexico's secretary of agriculture—began experimental work with sorghum. Their work began with the premise that drought-tolerant sorghum might help to resolve the problems of areas marginal for maize, those in which rainfall was either limited or poorly distributed (Pitner et al. 1954:1).

Early experiments did not meet with great success or with much interest among agriculturalists. It was only at the end of the 1950s that great interest in the grain was shown. In 1957, the Rockefeller Foundation annual report on the Mexican Agricultural Program reported:

> Interest in sorghums has grown considerably during the last year principally because of the rapid expansion of the livestock industry, especially pork and poultry production. As a result of recent heavy demand, the price of sorghum grain in Mexico City has increased from 400–450 pesos a metric ton at harvest time in 1955 to 790 pesos in May, 1957 (Rockefeller Foundation 1957:77).

Since 1958, when the government began collecting statistics on sorghum, the crop's history is nothing short of spectacular (Figure 2.1). During the period 1965–1980, when the area cultivated in the country grew at a rate of 1.5 percent per year, area cultivated in sorghum grew at a rate of 13 percent per year. By 1980, sorghum occupied over 1.5 million hectares, about one-fourth the area of maize and more than twice the area of wheat, the miracle crop of the first Green Revolution. In terms of the amount produced, sorghum's increase was even more rapid—18 percent per year. Today sorghum occupies the second largest area sown in Mexico, but, despite having become the fifth largest sorghum producer in the world, the country is not self-sufficient. In some recent years (e.g., 1983–1984), the country has had to import 50 percent or more of national production, making Mexico the second largest purchaser of sorghum from the United States.

The reasons for this green revolution in sorghum involve a combination of technological and ecological as well as socioeconomic factors. From the technological point of view, the production of sorghum in Mexico benefited from the creation of sorghum hybrids developed in Texas. Until 1955, the production of sorghum hybrids on a grand scale was not possible. With the discovery of male sterile plants, however, sorghum hybrid production increased so rapidly that by 1960 approximately 95 percent of the sorghum in the United States was sown with hybrid seed

(Quinby 1971:17–19). Mexican farmers quickly recognized the productivity of hybrids used by their neighbors to the north and began replacing maize with sorghum or introducing sorghum into newly opened areas. Thus, widely adaptable and highly productive hybrid sorghums from the United States were quickly adopted by an important group of relatively large-scale Mexican farmers *without* the benefit of national or international government programs to encourage production, *without* the sponsorship of any bilateral or multilateral aid agency, and *without* the teaching and technical assistance of any extension agents.

At the same time, transnational animal feed companies were transforming poultry- and pig-raising technology and creating a burgeoning demand for sorghum. In 1964, for example, Ralston Purina began a campaign promoting the benefits of sorghum, discussing the cultural practices necessary to grow it and providing hybrid seed from the United States to producers. Finally, the company offered to buy the total production on very attractive terms for use as an input in its diverse lines of nutritionally balanced livestock feeds.

DeKalb, Pioneer, Northrup-King, Asgrow, Funk, and other transnational seed companies, unencumbered by the laws regulating their activity in maize seed (see Barkin and Suárez 1983:102–107; Barkin and Suárez 1986; and Barkin 1987 for a discussion of these laws), responded to the demand for hybrid sorghum seed by establishing research and marketing operations in Mexico. These hybrids are basically the same high-yielding seeds bred for use as animal feed in the United States. Because virtually all of the sorghum in Mexico is planted using hybrid seed (Barkin and Suárez 1983), its adoption and use must surely qualify as one of the most successful cases of diffusion of innovation of all time (Rogers 1971).

Yields of sorghum in Mexico have been much higher than those of maize and reach nearly the average yield of wheat (Figure 2.2). Horacio Aburto (1979:145) found that under similar technological circumstances on irrigated land average yields of sorghum were 40 percent higher than those of maize. On rainfed lands, average yields of sorghum were 89 percent higher. Because agricultural scientists agree that maize has higher yield potential, its poor performance must be attributed to the failure of the national agricultural research and seed system to deliver a competitive variety or hybrid. These deficiencies are compounded by the relative lack of credit and the disadvantageous producer prices fixed for maize as compared to those prevailing in the much less regulated domestic market for sorghum.

Sorghum production has also benefited from infrastructural improvements. Although the Office of Special Studies originally experimented with sorghum for marginal lands, since 1970 about 35 percent of the sorghum was grown under irrigated conditions. Large extensions of land

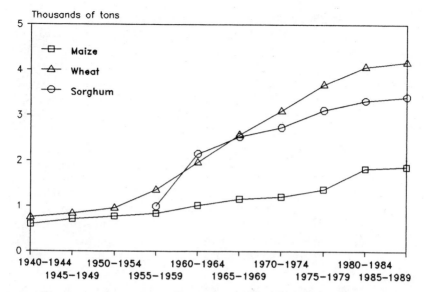

FIGURE 2.2 Yields of Maize, Wheat, and Sorghum, 1940–1989

Sources: SARH (Secretaría de Agricultura y Recursos Hidráulicos), *Estadísticas Básicas 1960–1986 para la Planeación del Desarrollo Rural Integral*, Mexico City: SARH, 1986; SARH, *Econotecnica Agrícola*, "Consumos Aparentes de Productos Agrícolas, 1925–1982," Vol. 7:9, Sept. 1983; Carlos Salinas de Gortari, *Primer Informe de Gobierno 1989*, Mexico City: Poder Ejecutivo Federal, 1989, Anexo.

in such productive irrigated zones as Tamaulipas, Sinaloa, and the Bajío (a highly productive area of central Mexico) are now planted in sorghum, in part because it requires less water than maize or wheat. In some regions of the country, like the Bajío, that have experienced droughts in recent years, the government has sometimes had to limit irrigation water because the reservoirs have been at low levels. Bajío farmers in 1982, for example, were allowed to irrigate only twice rather than four times as had been their practice. Under such conditions, sorghum has a definite advantage. While the drought that hit Mexico in 1982 reduced maize yields 40 percent below the previous year's levels (J. Walsh 1983:825), sorghum yields were not as drastically affected.

Sorghum has also benefited from the Mexican government's policies to encourage mechanization and the use of agricultural inputs. In most of the country sorghum cultivation is highly mechanized; tractors are used for plowing, seeding, and cultivating and combines are used for the harvest. Sorghum has thus been aided by the heavy subsidies accorded tractor production, operation, and purchase (Yates 1981:129). Even poor *ejidatarios* interviewed in the Bajío, San Luis Potosí, Sinaloa, Michoacán, Puebla, and Morelos use manual labor only in some hand weeding and in scaring away birds just before the harvest. All other operations are carried out by rented tractors and with combines contracted for harvesting. Hired trucks work in concert with the combines to carry the grain immediately to the granaries.

Sorghum has come to be seen by the farmer as a crop with many advantages compared with the relatively more labor-intensive maize, which requires between two and ten times as many person-days of labor per hectare. Sorghum cultivation is also a less risky undertaking because the grain is more drought-tolerant than other crops. In addition, farmers report there is little need to worry about "midnight harvests" of sorghum. In some areas, a substantial amount of the maize is stolen by passers-by; in contrast sorghum is not grown for human consumption in Mexico. The high degree of mechanization is also seen as an advantage by many smaller farmers, who have increasingly turned to off-farm employment opportunities to support themselves and their families (Roberts 1982, 1986). In one community that we studied in San Luis Potosí, for example, over 50 percent of *ejidatarios* had been to the United States to work as illegal migrants within the past five years. These individuals continue as part-time farmers in Mexico because very little of their own labor is required, allowing them to seek more remunerative work in other places (DeWalt and Barkin 1987).

The government price support system has also contributed significantly to make sorghum an attractive crop. The most rapid increases in sorghum production came in the mid-1960s. In fact, the amount of sorghum produced nearly doubled from about 747,000 tons in 1965 to over 1.4 million tons in 1966. This is the same period of time in which basic foodgrain production began to stagnate and decline (see corn acreage in Figure 2.1). This critical turning point in Mexican agriculture saw the confluence of two important government policy changes. The first was that, because of the high cost of the price supports, the government decided to freeze prices for most grains in 1962 and not to raise them again until 1973; the guarantee price for wheat actually dropped from 913 pesos to 800 pesos per ton. The second important policy change was the initiation of a guarantee price of 625 pesos per ton for sorghum in 1965. These two decisions made wheat and maize less profitable to grow while stimulating sorghum cultivation. Many farmers who had been growing wheat switched to sorghum or to other higher value cash crops (Hewitt de Alcántara 1976). A similar pattern emerged on a much larger scale among maize farmers. The price of sorghum has been between 58 percent and 84 percent of the price of maize during the last two decades (DGEA 1982). With its higher yields, lower production costs because of lower labor requirements, and reduced risk, sorghum has rapidly displaced maize.

Sorghum output would not have increased too spectacularly in Mexico, however, were it not for the steadily increasing demand from the animal feed industry. The number of establishments producing animal feed has grown explosively since 1975 as new feeding techniques displace traditional methods. A few transnational corporations like Ralston-Purina and Anderson-Clayton—along with a government competitor, ALBA-MEX—virtually control key ingredients in this industry (Barkin and Suárez 1985:135–136). Though productivity has risen dramatically, so have production costs, and the result is a higher relative price of pork and poultry products.

As indicated earlier, industrialized production of eggs, poultry, and hogs was the most dynamic sector in rural Mexico in the 1970s. Although the animal feed industry also uses maize, barley, wheat bran, soybeans, and other products, sorghum supplies 74 percent of the raw material used in animal feed in Mexico. The expansion of sorghum production, the emergence of the specialized feed industry, and the growth of poultry and hog production have gone hand in hand. The expansion of each has been made possible by the existence and growth of the others.

Despite the phenomenal growth of sorghum production, the country is still unable to grow enough to satisfy demand. In 1983, Mexico imported 3.3 million tons of sorghum, about 40 percent of the total utilized; this figure declined to 1.5 million in 1988, reflecting both an increase in sorghum production and a decline in internal demand for pork as a result of the deepening national economic crisis. Sorghum thus epitomizes the trends in Mexican agriculture toward *ganaderización* (livestock-oriented production) (Barkin 1981–1982). That is, a growing share of rural resources is devoted to fodder production for livestock to provide a high-protein diet for the minority wealthy and middle-class Mexicans, whose incomes increased much more rapidly than those of the rest of the population during the 1970s (Hardy 1982).

Enormous quantities of natural resources are devoted to the production of meat. The proportion of cultivated land devoted to animal production has gone from about 5 percent in 1960 to over 23 percent in 1980 (Barkin 1981–1982:66–67), while 64 percent of the national territory is used to produce just 3.1 million tons of meat in 1984, a yield of only 24 kilograms per hectare; in 1989, production declined to less than 2 million tons (Salinas de Gortari 1989:86–87). The proportion of grain fed to animals increased from 6 percent in 1960 (Meissner 1981) to over 32 percent in 1980 (DeWalt 1985a). The specialists at the National Food

Program estimated grain fed to animals to be as high as 48 percent of total apparent grain consumption in 1985 (*UnoMásUno*, January 9 and 10, 1985). (This is probably changing as meat consumption has declined more rapidly than real incomes with the implementation of a succession of austerity budgets in Mexico during the late 1980s.) The Mexican nutritionist Adolfo Chávez has likened this use of resources for meat production to the miracle that Christ performed with the loaves and the fishes—but in reverse (1982:9).

The social benefits of the use of cropland, grains, and the 74 million hectares of pasture are very poorly distributed. Although per capita consumption of meat is about 60 kilograms per year (DeWalt 1985a), the government itself reported that over 25 million Mexicans (more than 35 percent of the population) *never eat meat* and that less than 30 million drink milk regularly.[15] Although many occasionally consume animal products (eggs and milk), it is clear that the distribution of the products is sharply skewed toward the upper and middle income groups. Malnutrition is widely accepted to be one of the country's gravest public health problems; in 1979, the SAM reported that "more than 90% of the population suffers from caloric and protein underconsumption. . . . [About 40% of this group] have serious deficits which range from 25% to 40% of the minimum" (SAM 1980:8–9). Since that time nutritional standards have deteriorated substantially as real per capita incomes have plummeted more than 50 percent and un- and underemployment have become increasingly serious.

Obstacles to Development:
Government Policy and the World Market

On the surface, the profound changes in Mexican agriculture are results that any developing country would envy. Had they considered the situation from the perspective of 1940, policy makers would have predicted that the agricultural transformations just described would have solved the country's food problems. One-third of the cultivated area is now irrigated, the country has experienced technologically successful green revolutions in wheat (in which yields have quadrupled) and sorghum (which has become the second largest crop), per capita domestic production of grains is almost double the per capita grain utilization of the 1940–1944 period, and agricultural production has risen much faster than population growth (DeWalt 1985a).[16] Yet, one can still talk about an agricultural crisis in Mexico. More than one-half of the population is undernourished and imports of grain in 1989 were 10 million tons, more than 40 percent of national production. The question then becomes why has the transformation of Mexican agriculture—its successful modernization, to use the jargon of modern social science—not led to agricultural development and the solving of the country's food problems?

This pattern of agricultural growth without development is part of the broader process of economic modernization and integration into the world market. In all sectors, and in all social strata, traditional activities are being reorganized or displaced to make way for a new organization of production based on a growing monetarization of all aspects of economic life. Cooperative labor exchanges to produce crops are displaced by wage labor; purchased capital-intensive agricultural inputs replace labor-intensive forms of production; commercial animal feeds replace onsite consumption of household wastes, natural pastures, and other products unusable by humans; and processed foods and purchased commodities replace home production, processing, and use of basic foods. Consumption and distribution patterns, technology, and the organization of work and social life are all rapidly being transformed in the image of dominant trends in other countries, especially the United States.

The expansion of sorghum in Mexico is a dramatic example of the transformation of the way in which producers make decisions that create obstacles to further development. Instead of focusing on family or community needs, the farmer examines the increased *economic* productivity (or value) of new crops to determine their profitability. The modern inputs that are used to produce the crop allow profits for the providers of the seeds, machines, chemicals, and credit. Accumulation is also possible by those who transport the crop, by the processors who transform the grain into balanced livestock feed, by the entrepreneurs who use the feed to produce meat and other animal products, and by the butchers, supermarkets, and restaurants that finally deliver the product to the consumers. Producers' incomes depend on what remains after the suppliers and the buyers have imposed their conditions. The multiple factors involved in the sorghum boom included the conjunction of technological advance and change, government policies to encourage the modernization of agriculture, farmer decisions based on the greater economic productivity of sorghum, the increasing demand for livestock products, and the investments of transnational corporations and local entrepreneurs in "industrialized" production of feed and livestock.

The contrast of this new system with more traditional patterns of grain production and consumption is striking.[17] Historically, fewer inputs were used and fewer steps intervened between the crop and its ultimate use. Planting decisions were made on the basis of consumption needs rather than indirect market determinations, which may reflect conditions in other countries or speculative pressures by powerful actors in the market. Most small farmers must stick with their traditional systems and products for lack of resources to plant more profitable crops; many of those that do find nonagricultural alternatives abandon farming completely or relegate responsibility to other members of the family. Without credit and with restricted access to the institutional nexus that facilitates the adoption of new crops and techniques, most rural Mexicans cannot participate in the prosperity of agricultural modernization. Most technical observers acknowledge that a great many of these farmers could substantially raise output by using measured amounts of fertilizer and only marginally modifying present cultural practices; such changes are unlikely, however, without changes in macroeconomic policies to improve the relative prices (and profitability) of these grains and provide for credits to finance purchased inputs and living costs during the growing season, as is done in commercial agriculture (Redclift 1983; Felstehausen and Díaz-Cisneros 1985).

Modern producers have ceased to make planting decisions on the basis of family or community needs related to traditional patterns of specialization and consumption. With an increasing range of crops and access to credit, technical assistance, fertilizers, and other modern inputs, wealthier farmers now have much greater choice as to what they can produce and how to produce it. As information about world markets improves and national governments encourage export production, producers continually search for new, more profitable planting opportunities. The world market makes its impact felt in the midst of the family farm as producer prices adjust to reflect global changes, either autonomously through the market or with the intermediation of official policy makers. Local decisions are increasingly influenced by the relative profitability of alternative crops regardless of local or national needs. The crops that benefit from this mechanism are those commodities, such as sorghum and some fruits and vegetables, destined for export or for social groups with the highest and fastest growing incomes, rather than for the urban workers and rural population who make up the majority in third world countries.

The imbalance between internal demand and supply of basic foods for human consumption that has emerged is a predictable result of deliberate decisions. Government policy has encouraged crops destined for export markets or the plates of the middle classes; basic research and technological advances have reinforced this tendency.[18] The rapid growth in maize in the past few years is principally due to small farmers planting more area for on-farm consumption to compensate for declining monetary incomes. Thus, increasing maize production has not led to increased deliveries to the urban areas, which must be supplied by imports, because prices are too low to be a significant incentive for smallholders to produce for the market.

Thus, the seemingly contradictory statistics presented in this chapter reflect both market forces and government policies that condition decisions by Mexican farmers, processors, and businessmen. The rising Mexican middle- and upper-class demand for meat coincides with this new productive structure. The data also confirm the rationality of rural producers, who reduced marketable production as a reaction to systematic government efforts to maintain low prices for grains destined for human consumption in the hopes of stimulating further industrial investment and restraining urban wage demands (de Janvry 1981). As we have seen, this has left most production of maize and beans in the hands of a huge number of small agriculturalists who cultivate rainfed plots using relatively labor-intensive techniques. These smallholders increasingly find themselves with no alternative but to stop producing marketable surpluses or to abandon cultivation altogether; as a result, large extensions of land are no longer systematically cultivated and underemployment has become an increasing problem. Most commercial farmers do not find it profitable to produce basic grains, and thus devote larger and larger amounts of cropland to: (1) the production of agricultural commodities destined to be consumed by animals rather than directly by people, or (2) the production of high-valued fruits and vegetables for wealthy domestic consumers or for export. (Ironically, because of distorted distribution and pricing incentives, 1 million hectares of irrigated land are planted profitably with maize using intensive methods and hybrid seeds, but this area encompasses some of the country's most productive land and highly subsidized water, which might otherwise be available for even more profitable agro-export production.)

Furthermore, the distorted pattern of development of Mexican agriculture has resulted in a generalized move toward a demand-driven model of agricultural production. The "natural" shift toward crops with higher income elasticities of demand has imposed its own "modern" imprimatur on Mexican agriculture: a productive structure oriented toward animal feed, luxury foods, and agro-exports. Because of this, and in spite of the ready availability of the necessary human, natural, and produced resources, small farmers traditionally responsible for staple food production can no longer guarantee the country adequate supplies. As is evident from the history of sorghum in Mexico, neither the scarcity of official technical assistance nor insufficient knowledge of the potential benefits of new technologies is the primary obstacle to productivity increases. As elsewhere in the world, small farmers, like other producers, have shown themselves to be quite innovative and willing to change in response to new opportunities (Schultz 1964; DeWalt 1979; Eicher and Staatz 1984). But most small farmers in Mexico, and in other parts of the third world, find themselves unable to adopt the new technologies because inadequate private and public agricultural credit programs and misguided price policies make costly inputs of seeds, fertilizers, agro-chemicals, and machinery inaccessible. Small farmers are frequently unable to make their productive decisions on the basis of market signals; rather, they are driven to abandon cultivation or limit themselves to subsistence production that requires little or no monetary outlays but produces very low yields.

Most farming systems research demonstrates that small producers are aware of alternative cropping patterns or planting technologies that could increase yields and/or profitability. It also outlines the political mechanisms that exclude smallholders from participating in the process of agricultural modernization. Although farmers in the *ejido* sector control almost half of the cultivable land in Mexico, Susan Walsh has shown that they have consistently received less than 20 percent of the agricultural credit available (1984:114). With such lack of support, the fact that small farmers were producing as much as 38 percent of the total agricultural output as late as 1969 (Yates 1981:160) is a tribute to their tenacity and commitment. The official insistence on maintaining a combination of cheap food policies and lack of access to credit, which would permit small farmers to plant alternative crops or raise the productivity of traditional crops, has forced many *ejidatarios* to abandon their lands or to continue to plant food staples solely for subsistence needs rather than for the market. The result is that Mexico has been transformed into another food-deficit third world country, one of the largest.

Agricultural Development and Comparative Advantage

The growing imbalance between social needs and national production reflects one resolution to a long and heated debate over the formulation of official economic policy. Proponents of government intervention to formulate a national food self-sufficiency policy clashed with those who argued that international specialization, based on the principles of comparative advantage, was the best (most profitable) way to determine national production priorities and domestic policy.[19] Until the mid-1960s, there appeared to be a happy coincidence between the two criteria of need and profitability in many parts of rural Mexico. In the late 1960s, however, a dramatic policy conflict arose. The growth of Mexican agro-industry and the rapid opening of U.S. markets for Mexican exports of fruits, vegetables, and calves created new opportunities for wealthy farmers and ranchers (Sanderson 1984). Mexican and foreign private capital joined with state organizations to finance the new, more expensive technologies and infrastructure required to assure regular, export-quality crops.

The policy debate about rural development strategy continued to rage even after it was apparently resolved in favor of international specialization. Except for brief periods (1973–1975, 1980–1982), the foreign trade–based model of specialized commercial agriculture reigned supreme. Domestic price-support programs were said to strengthen small-scale agriculture by placing a floor under market prices for the crops produced by most small farmers. Since 1963, however, the crop price-support program ceased being used to stimulate basic food crop production and instead became a mechanism to reduce wage demands of urban workers by restraining inflation (Barkin and Esteva 1981). Higher world market prices determined the level of domestic prices for other crops and thus stimulated private investment in commercial agriculture. Government expenditures further exacerbated the gap between small-scale farmers and commercial farmers by providing infrastructure, credit, and technical assistance to commercial farmers to increase private profitability.

Some economists and many policy makers defended these trends by observing that this modernization has led to greater aggregate productivity in value terms and that it is not, *a priori*, disadvantageous for the country to import its basic food crops. The rationale for the Mexican situation, based on the theory of comparative advantage, is clear: Mexico is better off substituting the cultivation of higher valued products demanded by the wealthier classes within the country and/or by foreign consumers for the cultivation of staple food crops. The analysis supposes that after opening the sector to trade: (1) the small farmers would probably be better off, and (2) globally there would certainly be more goods produced, raising overall welfare levels. Thus, any objection to the pattern of development observed in Mexico would have to address the question of whether the application of the model of comparative advantage functioned as expected and who became the beneficiaries. In this section I examine the market imperfections prevalent in Mexico and common to most other third world countries that place these two fundamental assumptions in doubt.

The obstacles to the modernization of small-scale agriculture are substantial. The theory of comparative advantage predicts that such farmers will convert their resources to the production of more profitable crops or use more productive technologies to produce traditional foods. Throughout the country, innumerable studies (e.g., DeWalt 1979; 1985b) have documented the rapidity with which traditional communities typically adopt new crops and technologies when the communities' evaluation of the risks and benefits is favorable. But a majority of Mexico's small producers cannot participate in this process of productive transformation—as is now evident—due to lack of access to machinery and agrochemicals and to inadequate prices for their products. Local, regional, and national mechanisms of economic and political control have systematically channeled toward the wealthier farmers the benefits from all available credit and other official programs to support agricultural modernization.

Though the small farmers were the apparent beneficiaries of the agrarian reform, most of them have never been able to transform their parcels into modern productive units. This is not because of ignorance or "cultural resistance," as some analysts might suggest, but rather for want of the complementary materials and technical resources that would make such a transformation possible. In spite of innumerable government programs created precisely to aid agricultural modernization, the history of institutional intervention in Mexico demonstrates a definite socio-economic bias against the majority of poor farmers. Even when specific programs of governmental action were explicitly designed to face this problem head on, as was the case with CONASUPO (Compañía Nacional de Subsistencias Populares) in 1973 or the SAM in 1980, the net effect was not to structurally improve the lot of the peasants or facilitate their ability to participate in the process of agricultural modernization. Instead, such programs simply facilitated small-producer access to the market, but without creating permanent mechanisms to permit smallholders to adopt new technologies or sow more costly and profitable crops (Andrade and Blanc 1987). As a result, when the programs were withdrawn the farmers were worse off than before because they had access neither to the modern inputs nor to the seeds and cooperative labor arrangements that were the backbone of the traditional productive system.

A second issue related to the theory of comparative advantage is the net impact of such policies on Mexican welfare. The main problem with the use of the theory in the Mexican setting is that it assumes full employment of resources. In Mexico, as in other third world settings, this is probably the most vulnerable of the model's assumptions (Robinson 1979:102–103). Before applying the theory's dictates to the formulation of policy, it is essential to consider the implications of resource under-utilization because in Mexico both land and labor are not fully used.[20] Since staple food production has become unprofitable and alternative cropping patterns have not been an option for a substantial number of small farmers during recent years, smallholders have been forced to abandon their lands or sow them using traditional methods, which require little or no cash outlay and perpetuate low yields. In their search for cash incomes for basic survival, these producers have accelerated the pressure on the urban areas, swelled the ranks of the informal sector, and joined the large number of undocumented migrants trying to find employment in the United States.

Serious market imperfections on the consumption side also affect the analysis. Regional political bosses, allied with local merchants, generally control the marketing and transportation networks that redistribute food from central distribution points to local markets (Díaz Polanco and Guye Montalvon 1977:56–62). Thus, when food supplies are not available locally, these groups raise prices above official levels or those prevailing in other more competitive markets (primarily in urban areas where political control by official agencies is more effective). Thus, rural consumers and producers do not benefit from rising imports of staple foods; their only recourse is to increase their production of food grains for on-farm consumption, a phenomenon that explains recent increases in maize production in spite of disadvantageous producer prices. The benefits from trade that theoretically accrue to the nation do not reach most of the countryside; the lower prices occasioned by imports probably, however, have a direct welfare impact on some groups of low-income urban consumers. The government is keenly aware of this problem and has established direct distribution and sales programs that offer some respite by creating effective competition, but these programs affect only a small share of the target population—the politically vociferous.[21]

On the consumption side, therefore, the benefits from trade do not go to the rural small-scale producers, nor are these benefits available to compensate small farmers for their losses because of the inability of government agencies to distribute the benefits to the rural areas. Given the prevailing institutional situation in Mexico and other third world countries, the only way to directly assure adequate supplies of food at accessible prices for rural consumers is either to transform the rural population into producers of these products or to assure them direct access to state distribution channels for grain and other basic consumer goods, which would require subsidies.[22]

Conclusion

The major conclusion that can be drawn from the Mexican case is that *the modernization of agriculture through improved technology and through the application of the theory of comparative advantage has done little to resolve the problems of rural development or eliminate hunger.*[23] It has been most profitable for farmers to grow foods for those with the ability to pay. This means luxury foods like meat, dairy products, and fruits and vegetables are accorded priority by producers. Government policies have also favored the production of these same commodities because such commodities provide food for the politically articulate upper and middle classes or because they may be exported to earn scarce foreign exchange. The problem is that, as Joan Robinson has stated:

> Meeting demand is by no means the same thing as contributing to development. From the point of view of the market, money is money whoever spends it, for whatever purpose, but from the point of view of development, there is a great deal of difference between one kind of development and another (1979:87–88).

If the approach of reconverting rural consumers into producers had been adopted, as proposed by the SAM or National Food Program (PRONAL) (Austin and Esteva 1987), the nature of the present financial and debt crisis would probably be very different. Instead of forcing the massive dismissal of tens of thousands of people and the progressive abandonment of additional areas of land, with a consequent need to import food, the vicious cycle of modernization and impoverishment could have been reversed; more employment and additional food supplies would have induced demands for consumer goods and opportunities for employment in other industrial sectors. Instead, the austerity program adopted by the present government has reduced real incomes of most salaried workers, rural workers, and the people in the informal sectors, further accentuating the concentration of personal incomes and dramatically reducing consumption of basic foodstuffs among the most nutritionally vulnerable socioeconomic groups. The consequent waste of human and natural resources that is so evident in the unemployment and underemployment of labor, the undernutrition of large portions of the population, the massive decampment of rural people who move to the cities, and the squalid conditions of slum communities all attest to the failure of these policies, in which the wants of the rich minority have taken precedence over the needs of the poor majority.

The Mexican case demonstrates that policies of agricultural modernization will fail to provide for basic food needs unless these policies are accompanied by a corresponding *food* policy that will guarantee an adequate diet to the whole population. As Moises Behar has said, "If it is agreed that the fundamental role of any society is to ensure the well-being of all its members, including their adequate nutrition, then the presence of malnutrition to any significant extent must be interpreted as a failure of that society to perform effectively" (1976:142). Judged in these terms, Mexico's rural development policies have failed.

Notes

1. The term *food self-sufficiency* as used in this book refers to the country's ability to supply its population with basic foodstuffs from domestic production in sufficient quantities to achieve minimum nutritional standards. This definition contrasts with the concept of food security, which refers to a country's ability to supply its population with food regardless of the source.

2. Rodríguez contrasts domestic prices, including prices fixed through the government guarantee program, with the evolution of international prices and concludes that "the internal prices of basic foods have tended over the long term to follow international levels" (1979:97–98).

3. The SAM was an ambitious program to achieve national food self-sufficiency. Although it dramatically improved the incentives for basic food production and increased subsidies for consumption, it rapidly fell victim to the exigencies of crisis. See Austin and Esteva 1987, Luiselli Fernández 1986, and Spalding 1985 for alternative evaluations of the program.

4. Of course, the recent economic history of many Latin American countries recounts the rapid erosion of these gains. For a discussion of the impact of crisis on living standards in the Mexican situation see Chapters 5 and 6 of this book and the references cited therein.

5. For a discussion of the process of internationalization, see the case studies in Sanderson (1985) and Fröbel, Heinrichs, and Kreye (1979). Unfortunately, the second book gives the erroneous impression that the NIDL is the result of export production in the third world for the advanced capitalist countries, whereas most studies show that it is a product of the acceptance by these latecomers of productive structures and consumption patterns copied from the richer countries, often for internal use rather than for export.

6. Sorghum is a grain with many cultivation characteristics similar to maize. Traditional white varieties are grown in Africa and Central America as a food crop; as a result of agricultural experimentation, red hybrids were developed as an animal feed suitable to be grown in semi-arid conditions. These red hybrids are produced in Mexico and are harmful to humans if consumed directly.

7. An abundant literature on the Mexican rural development experience is readily available. For this reason I only summarize research findings that I and other scholars have amply documented, as evidenced in the writings cited in the Bibliography. This is not meant as an excuse for the lack of tables and other quantitative material included here, but rather to explain my choice to concentrate on the underlying forces that have produced the results summarized in this section.

8. *Ejidos* are communities of farmers who organized to receive and work the lands expropriated from the great estates after the Mexican Revolution. In the great majority of *ejidos*, land plots have been allocated to farmers who cultivate individually. Only a small percentage of *ejidos* operate communally.

9. Of course, the same technological approach was being employed in industry. Adopted in the postwar period, the import substitution–industrialization (ISI) model, which was the urban component of the "Mexican miracle" during the

era of stabilizing development (1958–1970), permitted a rapid growth in industrial employment but encouraged the progressive incorporation of the most advanced imported production and marketing techniques, which rapidly led to limitations on the sector's ability to continue to absorb workers. Since many of the durable consumer goods produced by these industries were unaccessible for the majority of Mexicans, who even now earn less than the minimum wage, the industries rapidly found their growth stymied by the limitations of the internal market. When they shifted their orientation to export markets, they had to invest in even more capital-intensive techniques, further exacerbating the employment problem.

10. S. Walsh (1984) has shown that the amount of credit available to private farms has always exceeded that available to *ejidatarios*. This has been especially true in recent times. She reported that, "Moreover, when the amount of credit available to private farmers leaped forward during the decade of the 1960s, agricultural credit to *ejidatarios* even declined, leaving the land reform sector at a serious disadvantage with respect to agricultural modernization and the adoption of new technology" (1984:113).

11. This is not to say that there is not extensive knowledge about alternative technologies that might provide animal feeds not directly competitive with human nutrition. Extensive research is conducted on alternative sources of animal feed and the more intensive use of agricultural waste products for food and other needs. Even with this knowledge, however, the powerful animal-feed industry prevents consideration of alternative technologies as long as the industry itself cannot find a profitable way to market the alternatives; the problem of farmer acceptance becomes a secondary one in this context of dominant market signals strongly pushing producers to reorganize their production in terms of the demands of the particular technology being proffered. For an in-depth discussion of this problem and its social consequences, see Suárez and Barkin (1990).

12. Beans are not, strictly speaking, a basic grain. They are often referred to as such, however, and are reported as basic grains by the Mexican government. This usage is adopted here.

13. This figure was reported in the national press, although the government is quite circumspect when discussing the problem. Development economists frequently point out that imports of food (or anything else) are not inherently undesirable. Rather, they argue that the issue is whether the resources used to produce this food could be more productively used to produce other goods. In Mexico, however, this is not the issue because a substantial part of the land available for food production is idle due to public policies that discourage its use; as a result, the small farmers must look elsewhere for employment. These issues are discussed at length in the last chapter of this book.

14. The years between 1981 and 1985 all showed a negative balance of trade for the agricultural sector; in 1986 the balance turned favorable, as the undervalued peso greatly stimulated export production and maize production increased as farmers increased their plantings for on-farm consumption in the face of declining opportunities for cash income and rising prices. The country imported 7 million tons or more of food products annually in the 1986–1988 period. In 1988 and

1989 the agricultural balance of trade turned negative again and there is little prospect of a reversal without a dramatic about-face in rural development policy, which does not seem to be in the offing. In 1989 food imports jumped to 10 million tons.

15. The situation has continued to deteriorate since the National Nutrition Institute surveys of the 1970s, which prompted the government to make such declarations (Redclift 1981:14). An extensive analysis of the nutritional situation in Mexico at that time is presented in COPLAMAR (1982) and is also available in various documents of the Sistema Alimentario Mexicano (SAM). For a more current evaluation of the nutrition picture in Mexico, see Livas and Miranda Mérida (1988) and Centro de Ecodesarrollo (1988).

16. Yates (1981:15) estimated that Mexican agriculture grew at a rate of 5.7 percent per year from 1940 to 1965. He estimates that this slowed to an average annual growth rate of slightly less than 2.6 percent between 1965 and 1980.

17. This is not to say that sorghum itself is prejudicial to the country. Instead, the manner in which sorghum has been used is a symptom of how agriculture, the economy, and the society have been restructured. In other circumstances, the greater productivity of the crop under marginal conditions could help to enrich Mexico and to better the standard of living of its inhabitants. Research to find sorghums appropriate for marginal lands that can be utilized both as an ingredient for animal feed as well as for direct human consumption and that can be grown using cultivation technologies already in the hands of small farmers (see DeWalt and DeWalt 1982) can be extraordinarily important for improving the utilization of land resources and the lot of small farmers.

18. For an analysis of how the Green Revolution resulted in a program that benefited the wealthy farmers in the rural world, see Pearse (1980). Jennings (1988) takes this analysis further by examining the impact of the research programs of the international agricultural research organizations with a case study of Mexico. Barkin and Suárez (1983) and Barkin (1987) provide a detailed discussion of the impact of new seed technologies on the productive structure in Mexican agriculture.

19. This debate raged in the national press in 1979 when the question of Mexico's joining the GATT (the international General Agreement on Tariffs and Trade) was opened for public discussion (Story 1982). Although the decision not to adhere appeared at the time to be a defeat for those wanting to open the Mexican economy rapidly to international competition, the subsequent dismantling of the protectionist barriers around imports and Mexico's adhesion to the GATT in 1986 demonstrated this hasty judgment to be erroneous.

20. Gregory's (1986) affirmation that Mexican labor markets are in balance may appear to contradict this assertion, but the present approach addresses the problem differently. I do not address the problem of whether labor markets are out of equilibria at present market prices: Clearly, substantial underemployment exists. Rather, given the present managed price structure for rural labor and the dearth of employment opportunities in Mexico, a remunerative price for basic grain production by small farmers would induce a substantial increase in the available labor supply to cultivate idle land.

21. The official statistics are provided by the Distribution Division of CONASUPO (DICONSA) and cover 51 percent and 66 percent of the rural and urban target groups (defined as low-income), respectively. The organization claims to have about a 5 percent share of the national retail food market, climbing to 22 percent in the case of maize and sugar and 17 percent for beans. For a summary of the government report see the lengthy five-part series of articles by Ricardo del Muro in the Mexican daily *UnoMásUno*, 30 December 1984–4 January 1985. The report itself was not made available to the public.

22. See Chapter 7 of this book for a lengthy exploration of this approach.

23. The history of sorghum production in Mexico is already beginning to repeat itself in countries like Brazil, Colombia, the Dominican Republic, Costa Rica, Panama, and others. Larger farmers are increasingly producing sorghum destined for consumption by animals. Yet, in many countries of Africa and in India, Central America, and Haiti, sorghum grown in marginal areas has great potential for use as a food for direct human consumption. The question becomes: Can research be reoriented from the development of methods favoring the use of modern technology for the production of luxury foods? My analysis points out the difficulty of achieving this goal. Technological advance does not, in and of itself, ensure that the benefits of that advance go to poorer farmers on marginal lands who are attempting to produce basic staples to feed themselves and those urban consumers who can afford only basic staples. The Mexican experience examined here suggests just the opposite.

3

Managed Environmental Decay

In March 1988, Mexico promulgated an ecology law that elevated a long history of declarations of good intentions to the level of formal commitments to confront the problems of the deteriorating quality of the natural environment. In the words of José María Alponte, one of Mexico's more astute journalists, this initiative reflected a "collective concern and political commitment" to confront the problems resulting from the historical assault of the productive apparatus on the natural environment. Alponte celebrated the event by noting, "For the first time, both the head and the heart know that the defense of our surroundings is also the defense of our development." But he also cautioned that "laws are never anything more than weapons that society might use" to advance its common weal (Alponte 1987).

This law is an achievement of the Undersecretariat of the Natural Environment (Subsecretaría del Medio Ambiente), a branch of the Ministry of Urban Development and Ecology (SEDUE). The ecology law establishes a legal basis for the ministry's mandate to reverse the systematic process of environmental degradation that has devastated Mexico during recent decades. The ministry's past efforts include eliminating particularly egregious sources of industrial pollution—including several paper mills and a chrome processing plant in the Valley of Mexico—and dealing with serious industrial accidents and mismanagement (such as the explosion of a gas processing plant in the northern part of Mexico City and the inadequate disposal of radioactive and other toxic wastes throughout the country). By its own admission, the SEDUE has been unable to meet most of these challenges, and the growing consciousness of the problems has created increased awareness of the ineffectiveness of present approaches to reversing environmental decline.

This chapter is a revised version of an article titled "Environmental Degradation and Productive Transformation in Mexico: The Contradictions of Crisis Management," published in the *Yearbook of the Conference of Latin Americanist Geographers, 1989*, Vol. 15 (forthcoming, 1990). Used by permission.

In this chapter, I examine the environmental problem in the context of Mexican development strategies. It is apparent that the concerted efforts of the economic authorities to confront the present economic crisis leave the rest of the policy apparatus with little room to maneuver in their own efforts to deal with other pressing social and environmental problems. Thus, as the gravity of the economic crisis increases, along with a new public awareness of its severity, new initiatives are being approved and even subsidized regardless of their environmental impact.[1] At the same time, ongoing programs designed to confront long-standing problems such as water treatment and waste disposal have been seriously cut back or even postponed because of the lack of financial resources *and* because of deep-rooted political opposition by vested interest groups who are presently charged with managing these areas.

The State's Role in Promoting Environmental Awareness

The Mexican state attempted to anticipate the environmental movement by encouraging the formation of special interest groups, which helped shape a framework for a state response to environmental problems. Not coincidentally, these new organizations were also instrumental in assisting the government to meet the demands that were being made for a coherent environmental policy by international banking and developmental agencies as a prerequisite for financial support. The activity of the state in this regard led it to participate in the formation of some groups while actively supporting the development of others. As was predictable, once formed, many of these groups assumed a life of their own, going beyond the narrow limits defined by their original conceptions or mandates. Such groups now regularly constitute an independent source of pressure for environmental policies, often in direct contradiction with the explicit wishes or interests of their original sponsors (Mumme et al. 1988).

Although the state played an active part in the forging of the incipient movement, the role of environmental activists should not be understated. Vigorous efforts by environmentalists were essential in creating national parks, wildlife preserves, and various other facilities, which promoted tourism and offered some permanent protection for a very small number of areas that were encompassed in these important but isolated initial efforts. In many instances, such as the duck hunting preserve in the northeastern part of the country (Tamaulipas) and the lake country in the southwest (Lagos de Montebello), the income generating potential from tourist activity was a decisive element in mobilizing local political forces to support international collaborative environmental demands,

Ducks Unlimited is one international group that participates actively in this program (see Figure 3.1 for the location of all place names mentioned in this chapter). Other efforts to protect natural or historical treasures—such as archeological ruins, natural caves and lakes, and the coastline—from the ravages of human organization have been only partially successful due to inadequate administrative and financial support and lack of a systematic staff training program.

But the Federal District is Mexico's single most serious problem, the one that continues to be the acid test of the official determination to resolve environment problems. Although it is generally acknowledged that a substantial proportion (some say as much as 80 percent) of all airborne contaminants in Mexico City comes from internal combustion engines, the large variety and volume of contaminants constitutes a profound challenge in any search for a solution. The problem of achieving citizen awareness and participation in understanding and searching for solutions has been left almost exclusively in the hands of ecology groups until perhaps the last two or three years. These groups have undertaken a number of campaigns on specific points of individual interest, especially related to the use of private automobiles, but no systematic program to involve the public in an understanding of or a balanced approach to the whole problem of pollution in the metropolitan area is at hand. A partial approach has begun: At last, mandatory emissions control testing was initiated in the Valley of Mexico in 1989, and 1991 model cars will come equipped with pollution control equipment long standard on export models.

Public agencies have been ill-equipped to tackle the whole range of issues concerning the quality of public services or to impose restrictions on private activities that contaminate the environment. Official policy was historically concerned with supplying the city with the basic public services required for survival: water, sewage and drainage, and garbage collection and disposal. There have been sporadic efforts to deal with the problems occasioned by the continual withdrawal of water from underground aquifers or from the contamination of the Xochimilco *chinampas* (cultivated islands). The partial reclamation of Texcoco Lake, in the east, is the result of the belated recognition of the impact of dust storms on the area's air quality. In addition, individual researchers have pointed out the serious effects of lead accumulations—resulting from high concentrations in fuels, paints, and other sources—on pre-natal and infant development.[2] These findings, along with some serious efforts at long-term planning, led to a redesigned collective transport system around an underground metro and a reshaped bus and trolley system, as well as a reformulation of the gasoline and diesel sold in the valley to reduce the content of lead and sulphur. As often is the case, however,

44

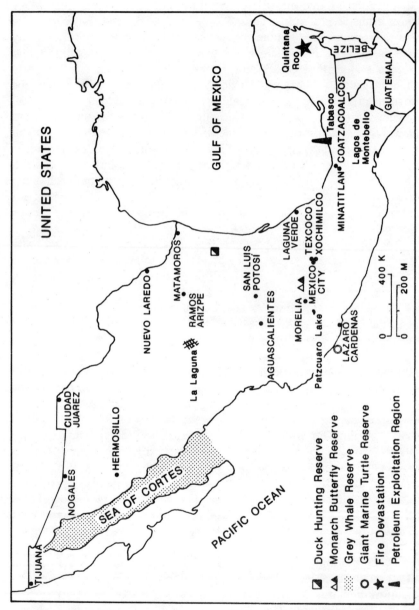

FIGURE 3.1 Principal sites of environmental concern

some of these solutions created problems as serious as—or more so than—the ones they were designed to solve.[3]

Unfortunately, the measures undertaken by the government have proved inadequate. Their greatest impact has been to gradually sow the seeds of greater public awareness of environmental problems; state intervention to correct some of the worst effects of environmental deterioration has been ineffective in reversing or even stemming the problem. And isolated individual demands and scattered programs by interested groups have also been ineffective. The situation has become so serious as to oblige the new (1988) Mexican president to declare environmental problems in the capital city as the highest priority for his administration.

The Conflict Between Productive and Environmental Imperatives

Mexico has demonstrated a fundamental inability to confront ecological imbalances in the face of other contradictions in the national development model. These contradictions are the result of a long history of competing demands on limited government resources to finance the development of private investment opportunities. These pressures historically have overwhelmed the popular (mass) demands for improvements in the quality of their material conditions. Profit-making activities have traditionally taken precedence over programs to enhance the natural environment or reduce inequalities in the social structure. In some cases the resolution was particularly cynical, as in the case of the decision in the early 1950s to postpone undertaking a systematic program to improve drinking water systems in rural Mexico and instead subsidize the sale of sugar to the soft drink manufacturers.[4] But in most cases, such "externalities" (as economists are wont to call environmental concerns) were simply neglected.

The conflict is most apparent when evaluating some of the environmental programs themselves. The most evident source of discord is the thermonuclear electricity generation plant at Laguna Verde in the state of Veracruz. This plant, using obsolete heavy water technology and hardware no longer considered commercially or politically acceptable in most parts of the world, was placed "on-stream" in late 1988. The antinuclear movement aroused a great deal of opposition to the plant (the movement's previous success in achieving the cancellation of a projected research reactor on Lake Patzcuaro created a momentum that is still evident). In response to the opposition from professional and citizen groups, the government resorted to a poorly regarded series of maneuvers, including visits by international expert groups, to proclaim the plant's technical integrity and safety to the nation, while skirting the issue of efficiency by pointing to the need for vast quantities of new power to supply the country with its basic needs. The even more serious problem of radioactive waste disposal appears to have been shrugged off. Alternative proposals, such as fueling the plant with natural gas from petroleum wells, which is presently flared for lack of adequate infrastructure to move it to market, were dismissed as unworkable. Some officials are also saying that the government is proceeding with its plans to build several more nuclear generating plants before the end of the century. However, such plans seem to be more expressions of hope (or defiance) rather than realistic goals, given the profundity of the economic woes that will be faced by Mexico during the coming decade.

The Plan of 100 Actions, promulgated in 1986, was directed in large measure to the capital city (Comisión Nacional de Ecología, SEDUE, 1987). The program called for the decentralization of some particularly contaminating industries and for a voluntary program of citizen and industry collaboration to stem the increasing concentration of pollutants in the Mexico City Valley. The plan also envisioned a broad-ranging series of measures to manage other environmental targets: It proposed to correct problems related to soil and water contamination in dozens of areas; it named eleven programs to create sanctuaries and biosphere reserves for the protection of natural resources and endangered species; and it committed the government to control the use of agrochemicals and regulate the formulation of detergents, as well as undertaking an ambitious program to establish more effective norms for evaluating the impact of these inputs.

The plan's practicality is perhaps most effectively questioned by the experience of the 1988–1989 winter in Mexico City. The government was unable to stem productive activities in industry or the use of private transport by the populace in spite of the highest measured levels of contaminants in the air of any urban area in recorded history. By its own lax standards, the city was declared to be in an emergency situation on an alarming number of occasions. Among the measures implemented in the framework of the plan were the highly disruptive program of extending the school year by canceling primary and secondary school attendance during January, the height of the period of thermal inversions, and a related attempt to stagger working hours. Neither program was thorough enough or coordinated well enough with the structure of other activities in the metropolitan area to be an effective countermeasure. Further complicating the task of reducing pollution is the inability of the responsible authorities to effectively modify the (foreign) design of the motors in public buses to reduce emissions or to modify automotive exhaust systems to more completely burn the new lower lead–content fuels introduced into the Valley of Mexico. The newly promulgated mandatory automotive inspection schemes and staggered withdrawal of private automobiles from circulation during the height of the winter crisis period are still quite inadequate.

Another related area of policy to improve environmental conditions in the Mexico City Valley is the announced commitment to decentralizing the government bureaucracy itself. Official declarations notwithstanding, only about 30,000 bureaucratic positions (of a total of more than 2 million) have actually been transferred from the metropolitan area. This is far less than the cutbacks in total government employment (nationally) of more than 50,000 imposed by the austerity measures of the national economic stabilization efforts of recent years.

These official centralized programs of corrective measures floundered on the shoals of fiscal austerity. The vast array of programmatic efforts to deal with soil and water contamination were postponed or delayed as the financial crisis deepened. In its stead, some sources of pollution disappeared as production declined with the severe reduction in purchasing power, but most pollution has simply continued to expand even faster than urban growth while the lack of concern with environmental side effects takes its toll on the quality of life throughout the country.

Much more effective than these official attempts is the impressive market-driven process of decentralization that has been observed in the 1980s. The border development program, based on labor-intensive manufacturing assembly operations and the southward flow of agribusiness from California (spurred by sharp devaluations of the peso), have created new development poles in northern Mexico. In the interior, new export industries have located in such cities as San Luis Potosí, Aguascalientes, Hermosillo, and Ramos Arizpe (among others) in response to effective industrial park schemes and other incentives. Clearly, private enterprise is contributing to a geographic reordering of the productive map of Mexico. But geographic decentralization has not reduced the problem of the contaminating impact of these industries on their new locations or on the people employed in the plants; it simply transfers this impact to new regions and imposes it on new social groups.

The Environmental Costs of
Industrial Development

There is a belated recognition that many solutions to environmental problems are at variance with the prevailing pattern of concentrated, export-oriented development. There is an inability to confront these environmental problems when they impose costs on private investors and a lack of resources to resolve them when they require public funds. New industrial projects, like the expanding petrochemical complex on the Gulf Coast, are being designed without regard to environmental consequences. It seems extraordinary that, even now, new businesses are allowed to establish in the Valley of Mexico, further attracting population and increasing demand for overtaxed public services. Elsewhere, new productive investments are having deleterious environmental effects, which are deepening the impact of the broader economic crisis on living standards by reducing the quality of life in many of the rapid growth poles of the country. Illustrative of such projects is the industrial complex at Ciudad Lázaro Cárdenas near the Pacific Coast in Michoacán that is being expanded to enlarge the capacity of the steel and fertilizer plants and to include new capital equipment manufacturing facilities (Restrepo 1984). These expansions are being financed by direct foreign investment as well as by loans from multinational lending institutions. New industrial ports are also spawning new centers of urban blight while wreaking havoc with the coastal regions and the sea in the areas in which the ports are being constructed.

Throughout the country the conflicts between productive demands and the health of workers and neighbors are becoming more apparent as researchers delve into these issues. One recent study pinpointed the deleterious impact of assembly operations on women workers in the Nogales area by studying the birth weights of their children, a measure widely accepted as an excellent indicator of the health of the mother. On the basis of a sample of several hundred women, the study concluded that toxic materials and physical demands made on workers at the assembly plants seriously debilitated them, leading to a dramatically higher incidence of lower birth weights (triple the incidence of the control group).[5] Other researchers have suggested that one of the major motivations for "runaway" shops—firms escaping from traditional manufacturing centers in the rich countries—is the great laxity with which worker health protection measures are enforced in many labor-intensive manufacturing assembly areas.[6] Incipient research on industrial accidents in Mexico points to a similar disregard of the problem on a much wider scope than occurs in the export assembly operations. The problem of pesticide use and the systematic neglect of even the most common safeguards have been widely documented (Wright 1986; Restrepo with Franco 1988).

The conflict between the exploitation of the nation's natural resources and the need to protect its natural heritage is a common theme among ecology groups. Perhaps one of the most tragic testimonies to the inability to resolve this problem adequately is in the area of forestry. Mexico has the world's sixth largest forest reserves but individual poverty and corporate greed have combined to denude the country of its varied forests without offering any reasonable alternative approach for creating a process of sustainable cuts to rationally exploit this renewable resource (Halhead 1984). As a result, the country imports large volumes of wood products for direct use and for processing into paper. In 1989, however, the lack of care of the nation's forests turned tragic as more than 130,000 hectares in the state of Quintana Roo on the Yucatan Peninsula were decimated by fires that could have been controlled, had early warnings been heeded and preventive measures implemented. The damage to local flora and fauna is incalculable and further threatens a fragile ecosystem. Similar problems have emerged with regard to the nation's hydraulic resources, including the underground aquifers on the Pacific Coast and in the Sierra Madre that are the source of water for many hydroelectric plants and hundreds of thousands of hectares of the most fertile cultivated lands. These underground aquifers are being depleted and contaminated at a rate that threatens the very continuity of the productive activities that depend on them.

The government's inability and/or unwillingness to deal with these problems in a serious way is nowhere more evident than in the area of waste disposal. Examples range from the heinous to the mundane. There is the dramatic case of the theft of a container holding radioactive cobalt-60 pellets in an apparatus for medical diagnosis in Ciudad Juárez that was purchased by public health authorities but left unsecured. Once the machine was vandalized and sold for scrap, the remains were deposited in an open-air landfill; even after the problem was identified, no satisfactory measures were taken until international press coverage made it the subject of an international scandal.[7] Venality and incompetence have combined with bureaucratic indifference to convert this incident into an all too common occurrence: U.S. toxic waste disposal companies have frequently been discovered "red-handed" crossing the border with forbidden cargoes, misinforming customs agents, and buying the right to dispose of their loads in Mexican garbage dumps.

But even within the country, commercial and citizen participation in garbage disposal and recycling are virtually forbidden topics. When the Centro de Ecodesarrollo conducted a survey of the content of garbage and the nature of its disposal in Mexico City, practically every public school child in junior high school visited the public exposition of the results (presented in the city's Technological Museum), but attempts to channel these efforts into a serious discussion of how to deal with the problem have floundered (Restrepo and Phillips 1982). More recent marketing innovations such as the packaging of beer and soft drinks in cans and nonreturnable bottles are widely advertised as major advances, although their real cost to the consumer and to society is still not a permissible theme for polite conversation, especially in the SEDUE. Any reform efforts in this realm and others must confront vested political and economic interests that control solid waste disposal, sewage treatment, and recycling in general.

Popular Efforts to Deal with Local Problems

Citizen awareness of environmental decay is relatively undeveloped in Mexico. There seems to be a pervasive attitude that the area outside one's own home is the responsibility of the government. Willingness to deal with littering and public cleanliness in general (including that in public restrooms) is stymied not so much by ignorance as by a lack of resources and by collective indifference. Public waste barrels are scarce, at best, but more garbage barrels will not deal with the problem as long as the formal waste collection systems are inadequate. The absence of adequate sewage systems and treatment plants complicates the sanitation problem. In the face of individual poverty and apathy these collective failings create often insurmountable barriers to resolving even the most basic problems. It is not surprising that there is virtually no open discussion of these crucial problems.

An urban-based ecology movement has emerged to champion a few causes. As mentioned at the beginning of this chapter, some of these efforts were initiated or at least protected by the very government authorities who were to be influenced by the lobbying efforts. Most of these ecology groups are based in the capital and attempt to stimulate mass participation in improving the urban environment. They have concentrated on neighborhood projects (parks, trees) and issues surrounding the private automobile. Their success has been limited and their impact in other parts of the country, virtually nil. The largest single activity of these groups was focused on organizing a mass resistance to the nuclear power plant. Although it was successful in delaying the project, the movement doomed itself by not planning a series of alternative activities for the moment when the inevitable decision to make the plant operational was taken.

The most effective nongovernmental efforts involved the collaboration of Mexican groups with interested parties from abroad. Two of the best known were by organizations that worked to create biosphere reserves to protect the natural habitats for long-distance migratory species: the gray whale (Baja California and the Sea of Cortés) and the Monarch butterfly (Michoacán). Both reserves have led to a flourishing tourist trade, bringing thousands of visitors to enjoy the natural occurrence while providing a growing measure of protection to the species that come to Mexico as part of their regular migratory cycle. But the wealth of many of the visitors compares starkly with the poverty of the people living in the affected areas and the small recompense they receive for reorganizing their societies as part of the effort to maintain the reserves. In Michoacán, the local residents have received potable water and electricity services, along with improvements in the narrow dirt road that serves the area. But they have neither the experience nor the resources to organize the process and construct tourist facilities so that they might improve the quality of the visit for outsiders, create more employment, and capture a slightly greater proportion of the expenditures. As a result, there are many doubts about the long-term viability of the program.

A similar effort to study and protect the giant marine turtle is being developed along the Pacific beaches of Mexico (Alvarado and Figueroa 1988). In Michoacán, the organizers are concerned with strengthening the project by integrating the local people into the effort; they are designing new productive activities to replace the local hunt for turtles. With this in mind, scientists are investigating the possibility of creating a new industry—iguana farms—as an alternative source of employment and income. They are also trying to anticipate efforts to integrate this protected area into the national tourist campaign by developing a new concept of "ecological tourism" that would be compatible with their efforts to protect the biosphere reserve while creating alternative sources of sustenance for the communities that must, in the final analysis, be the social basis for the protection effort. This project, still in its conceptual stages, illustrates the possibilities for such development but also the difficulties that local organizations will encounter when trying to find alternatives within the framework of the existing organization of pro- duction.

The SEDUE (1987) provides a long list of other projects that have enjoyed local participation by diverse producer and citizen groups. This list includes 147 firms that have agreed to a series of measures to reduce their harmful impact on the environment. In addition, SEDUE's reports mention a large number of other steps taken in collaboration with interested groups, local authorities, and international organizations to protect endangered species, create natural reserves, or undertake direct action to resolve pressing health problems. One well-publicized example of the ministry's efforts to involve local communities in the solution of their own problems is a project to filter arsenic and other salts out of water contaminated by agricultural activities. The program created a number of permanent jobs and guarantees a permanent supply of high- quality bottled water for the region. Unfortunately, however, even in the exhaustive list of its own actions, the SEDUE provides little evidence of a concerted effort to correct the profound environmental distortions created by the pattern of economic development during recent decades. Its actions have not contributed to the redesign of production facilities.

Interestingly enough, many local projects are not mentioned by the ministry. These include reforestation programs and various other efforts to find productive uses for resources that will also help reduce ecological deterioration. Although in many cases the problems are quite serious and widely recognized, the corrective efforts are generally inadequate. Such is the case of the many-faceted effort of the state petroleum company to confront the broad swath of destruction its crews have carved out of the tropical regions and Gulf Coast of Mexico (Barkin 1978; Toledo 1983; Beltrán 1985).[8] The "Green Campaign," splashed across the media by PEMEX (Petroleos Mexicanos, the state-owned petroleum company), seems as incongruous and insensitive as the billboards, mounted on flatbeds and pulled along Mexico City's major arteries by tractor-trucks, to sell products and boast of the sponsor's commitment to improve the environment while asking people to drive more courteously. In Tijuana and other border towns, local problems have acquired an international dimension and binational committees are attempting to reduce the release of contaminated waters.[9] Less progress is being made in dealing with solid waste disposal in these border areas because the dumps do not cross international borders.

In the Lake Patzcuaro area of Michoacán a high degree of consciousness about the region's problems was developed during the past decade. Concern about the dumping of raw sewage and the erosion of vast volumes of topsoil into the lake led to the search for corrective programs. One program, sponsored by local environmental groups in conjunction with official agencies and funded in part with international support, involved the terracing of a large area and the planting of peach trees in the region. The program sparked the imagination of many groups and has proceeded apace since 1983. As the works advance and the trees mature, however, it is becoming increasingly evident that the original criticisms about the approach and the technical design were well founded: It appears that the fruit trees are inappropriate for the region and that local wind patterns will condemn the fruit to not mature correctly.[10] Furthermore, the terraces were not designed to deal effectively with the magnitude of the problem in the Patzcuaro region. As a result the program appears doomed to be unable to correct the problems it was designed to attack while gradually undermining the enthusiasm and support of local groups. On a regional level, government red tape and budgetary limitations, along with a lack of determination by local leaders, continues to delay the installation of the primary sewage treatment plant needed for the region.

The Declining Prospects
for Environmental Improvement

In the midst of crisis, it is unlikely that Mexico's long history of inaction on environmental issues will be modified. Declarations of good intentions have rarely been reinforced with the needed financial resources. New productive programs are presently being approved without regard to their impact on their surroundings because other pressing problems have thrust such concerns from the list of priorities.

There are exceptions to this bleak outlook. In the case of those local groups determined and able to mobilize local opinion, effort, and resources (or foreign support), the inaction of central authorities and the rhetorical commitment to confront the problem provide opportunities to advance. This was how the program to build a sewage treatment plant in Tijuana prospered. Similar dynamics favor the turtle program in Michoacán. In the absence of resources, the government has facilitated such efforts by imposing fewer barriers. Unfortunately, as the Patzcuaro experience suggests, such local efforts are often plagued by lack of expertise and bad designs that only compound the problems created by corruption and greed.

The list of pending issues is long and the crisis will further lengthen it. The mundane problems of sewage treatment and solid waste disposal are sure targets of budgetary austerity programs. The ready alternative of declaring decaying lakes dead (as is being done in the Ciénaga de Cuitzeo near Morelia) has made it possible for local officials to declare themselves incapable of dealing with complex local problems, while higher levels of government are washing their hands of environmental issues because of budgetary restrictions and political convenience. The avowed intention to curb dangerous agrochemical use in the countryside has been rendered unenforceable because the appropriate authorities lack the resources and will to impose production restrictions on the most influential group of farmers in the country. No effective measures have been taken in the face of the recognition of the mortal danger of waste from hog raising to the whole population because cysticercos (which can cause mortal brain lesions) invade fruits and vegetables through irrigation systems. Nor have any advances been made to halt the use of lead-sealed cans for foods or even for those particularly aimed at children. Beer and soft drink producers compete with each other to introduce disposable bottles and cans while these containers dot the countryside, and no move has been made to even define the country's garbage dumps.

But the contradictions of the Mexican model of development go much deeper than these particularly visible scars. Workplace health and safety problems have not yet even been fully identified. The permanent damage from the many forms of pollution in the workplace and the community is just beginning to be understood. Furthermore, in spite of much lower per capita alcohol consumption in Mexico than in such European countries as France and Spain, the material and human losses from drinking are much greater.[11] These contradictions reflect the high degree of control exercised by important economic power groups over the bureaucracies that are supposed to regulate them and protect the interests of society.

The present development model, which privileges large-scale export manufacture at the expense of all else, provides no effective means to reverse the tendency toward environmental decay. Industry will not, unless obliged by government regulation, integrate a social conscience into its calculation of profit and loss. In Mexico the state has shown itself unwilling to impose the costs of environmental controls on production, lest the drive for successful export promotion be thwarted. Some people argue that small-scale industry and agricultural production may be more consistent with an environmentally sound pattern of development, but such considerations seem beside the point at a time when macroeconomic policy has decimated small industrial firms and converted the country into a net importer of food, leaving millions of hectares of land and millions of people idle. Official policy offers no solace in this regard: In place of a concrete set of programs to deal with the impending environmental crisis, the president only implores the "civil society" to raise its level of collective conscience. And what shall be asked of the producers?

Notes

1. One of the notable features of crisis management in Mexico has been the extraordinary ability of the government to convince the people of its competence to restore the economy to an upward path in a short period of time, despite a real compression of personal incomes greater than that that occurred during the height of the military dictatorships in each of the southern cone countries (Argentina, Brazil, and Chile). Until the July 1988 elections the Mexican people did not appear to have lost confidence in the state's ability to administer the economy. Since the imposition of the most recent austerity measures, with the continuing fall in real wages and the deepening of the economic crisis, the political situation has continued to deteriorate. For more on this see Chapter 6 of this book.

2. Ironically, more information about this research is available outside Mexico than in the country. William Branigin of the *Washington Post* (28 November 1988) reported at great length on the effects of lead, including a survey of the major researchers examining the problem. In Mexico, this information is only available to the most specialized of interested groups.

3. For example, the introduction of new gasoline formulations has intensified the concentration of ozone (now the most important contaminant) in Mexico City's air. Another modification of gasolines sold in the valley, lowering the lead content and raising the octane rating to assure fuller combustion by adding imported compounds to the fuel, became available in late 1989.

4. This assertion of the use of a subsidy for soft drinks is based on conversations with policy makers in the pertinent ministries. There is no published documentation to substantiate it.

5. Denman (1990) reports that this significant difference did not arise from nutritional deficiencies of the women in the study group. The study found that a large proportion of the babies had low birth weights because they were premature rather than underweight full-term babies, as was the case in the control group.

6. This is a major point of the Emmy-winning film by Fernández-Kelly and Grey (1986). This film is based on research by a group of sociologists and anthropologists in Mexico and the Philippines. See also Fernández-Kelly (1983).

7. The incident was discovered when a pickup truck that had been used to carry some contaminated reinforcing bars was detected by sensors in the White Sands Proving Grounds (New Mexico) some time later.

8. Toledo (1983) points out that the injurious impact of petroleum development could not be avoided because the program : (1) attempted to dissociate production from its impact on the environment; (2) was predicated on the supposition of unlimited supplies of natural resources; and (3) did not attempt to understand or measure its ecological costs.

9. A long-term effort to implement a new technology capable of dealing with the needs for sewage treatment is being evaluated in Tijuana with financial assistance from the California Coastal Commission and the World Wildlife Fund. For more details on this see the work conducted by Ing. Carlos de la Parra and his colleagues based at El Colegio de La Frontera Norte, Tijuana.

10. The fruit trees were said to have been sold to the project at very high prices by one of the officials of the Ministry of Agriculture charged with administering the program.

11. Recent studies reveal that cirrhotic illnesses in Mexico are more frequent than in countries with higher alcohol consumption, suggesting a greater concentration of consumption in a smaller proportion of the population. The social and private cost of alcoholism in Mexico (as measured by damage to property, absenteeism, lowered productivity, and personal injury and illness) is also estimated to be quite substantial (Menéndez 1989).

4

Smuggling, Capital Flight, and Development Finance

In Mexico, as in many countries in the third world, capital flight continues unabated. It is a tangible way for the wealthy to demonstrate their lack of satisfaction with the existing state of affairs. As external pressures on the economy increase and confidence in the ability of national authorities to manage the domestic economy declines, it is predictable that both individual and corporate investors would seek to protect themselves from domestic chaos by transferring their wealth to safer havens. Even when they are interested in investing in their own countries, many wealthy people find that they can improve the conditions for their investments by investing as foreigners.

What is capital flight and why is it important? Capital flight is the departure from a given country of investable resources. Under normal circumstances this might simply be called foreign investment, but in the developing world, where one of the main imperatives for economic progress is further investment, any attempt to reduce investable resources must be understood as a vote of no-confidence in the economic future of the country. Thus, the massive exodus of capital contributes to a country's inability to broaden and modernize its productive apparatus. As I shall argue at the end of this chapter, capital flight not only undermines a country's ability to grow, but, perhaps even more insidious, it also contributes to a misunderstanding of the country's economic potential.

The flight of capital is a response by wealthy people to their discomfort with the prevailing economic environment. In practice, it is both a symptom and a weapon of class conflict. As a symptom, it is a vivid measure of an unwillingness to strengthen the economy through investment and the import of necessary goods and services; as a weapon, it represents a denial of resources for further growth. Analogous to foreign investment, which contributes an increase in real productive capacity, the emigration of important volumes of capital reduces a country's productive potential. But in contrast to the case of foreign investment by the wealthy from the industrialized countries, capital owned by the wealthy from the third world does not usually contribute to a future inflow of income from foreign investment to the country of origin: The lack of confidence that provoked the capital flight in the first place also leads the wealthy to retain their earnings abroad. Furthermore, since the rich typically amassed their wealth by employing people and resources within the country, this capital flight represents not simply the appropriation of valuable resources by a small group of people but the withdrawal of savings and foreign exchange, which are then no longer available for the country's future development. If the country could use the resources that were sent abroad, then it would be able to invest more and borrow less to promote an internal process of economic growth.

The international banking community has long been aware of this problem, and recent studies have begun to document its growing seriousness. Since much of this capital flight has gone to the United States, it may be that the United States remained unmoved to even recognize the problem because the massive unrequited inflows of funds allowed it to postpone confronting its own growing deficit in foreign trade, especially in the period since the heightening of the international debt crisis in 1982. The data suggest that for some countries, including the largest debtor nations, this capital flight was actually the cause for much of the increase in foreign debt: In Mexico, a reputable estimate of total capital flight places it at $53.4 billion, or 60 percent of the increase in external debt ($88.5 billion) during the 1971–1985 period.[1] In simple terms, the increase in foreign debt in many countries has been used to finance the accumulation of private wealth abroad by a privileged few. Even more starkly, if the returns from these foreign holdings by nationals in countries like Mexico could be made available for international economic obligations, it would be possible to virtually eliminate the problem of service on the external debt. In one simulation exercise, Manuel Pastor (1988) estimated that if one-half of these earnings were repatriated, economic growth in Mexico could have proceeded at perhaps twice its actual rate during the 1971–1985 period.

Smuggling and Capital Flight

Troubling as these estimates of capital flight based on reported flows are, they probably understate the problem. Detailed studies of foreign trade suggest that the practice of misreporting of the value of exports and imports is frequently used as another vehicle for expatriating capital, especially from economically unstable countries. This phenomenon is known as the "global current-account discrepancy." In more precise terms, this discrepancy is the result of unreconciled differences in reports of the value of commodities and services exchanged between trading partners. The current-account discrepancy between countries with weak economies and their principal trading partners has evolved as one might predict on the basis of a model of market reactions to perceived risk and anticipated yields: As risk from exchange rate fluctuations increased and expected real yields on domestic savings declined, surreptitious forms of capital flight increased (McDonald 1985). Since 1969, the global current-account discrepancy has grown from virtually nothing to represent some $39 billion on trade account and $74.8 billion for invisibles in 1980 (Veil 1982). In the measured voice of Erwin Veil, analyst from the Organization for Economic Cooperation and Development (OECD), these data suggest "that there may be serious deficiencies in recorded data" (p. 46). Similar concerns have been expressed by analysts at the International Monetary Fund and the World Bank (De Wulf 1981; Khan and Ul Haque 1985; McDonald 1985; Cuddington 1986). As recognition of the problem becomes more widespread, journalistic reports accumulate alongside careful academic analyses to confirm that a significant part of the global deficit is a private response to attempts by policy makers in many countries to limit the autonomy of traders and investors. For example, *Le Monde* (23 April 1985, p. 1) reported on the mechanisms used by Turkish traders to accumulate foreign exchange, and detailed interviews have revealed the systems developed by Mexicans with residences in southern California to extract hundreds of millions of dollars from their home country, often with subsidies from the government banking system, which offers credits to promote exports and finance necessary imports (*Wall Street Journal*, 11 October 1985; de Murguía 1986).

Capital Flight and Development Finance

Conventional thinking about economic development rests on the concepts advanced more than two decades ago by Hollis Chenery and his colleagues (Chenery and Bruno 1962; Chenery and Strout 1966). Their formulation of the two-gap model of national development demonstrated that progress was restricted by two gaps: an insufficient national savings capacity and the inability to generate adequate foreign exchange. Stephan Linder (1967) carried the analysis even further, suggesting that the persistence of the two gaps requires a thorough revision of orthodox development thought and theory up to that time. Although modeling has become more complicated since then, much of international economic and financial policy making is presently concerned with the problems of balancing domestic development programs with available supplies of savings and foreign exchange.

This approach is central to development policy in many developing countries. Throughout the third world, foreign debt was contracted to finance programs designed to *temporarily* resolve pressing problems of underdevelopment and postpone the need to search for internal solutions. Internal debates frequently focus on whether government revenues and these external resources were used effectively. Until recently, few responsible groups in those countries with weak currencies have seriously challenged the notion that their nation's problems are founded on its inability to generate sufficient internal savings or foreign exchange to finance even a minimally acceptable level of economic growth.[2] But both the analysis and the policy implication that a country has no alternative to foreign finance may be seriously flawed if present systems of reporting foreign trade and capital flows are permitting results with distortions as large as some of the aggregate analyses suggest.

Capital flight exacerbates economic management problems in both debtor and creditor nations. Because the governments of the debtor nations are deprived of the resources needed to finance international obligations and domestic investment, there is growing pressure to compensate for this loss by increasing taxes and prices on public sector goods and services and by cutting back on domestic development projects as part of an overall austerity program. Capital flight also induces changes in the price system by reallocating resources as people invest in those sectors and regions from which capital can be readily exported. These modifications in the price system, in turn, lead to unanticipated and undesirable changes in the productive structure.[3] Furthermore, by contributing to an underestimation of available savings capacity and to an overestimation of foreign exchange requirements, which must be financed by borrowing, capital flight contributes to a mistaken assessment of a country's productive potential. It also leads to an internal redistribution of income and welfare away from the broad majority, who are ravaged by currency depreciation, inflation, and additional governmental austerity programs, toward a privileged group that prospers by accumulating funds outside the country.

The creditor nations are troubled by the flight of capital because the financial solvency of a debtor nation determines its ability to continue to fulfill its commitments to service outstanding debt. Although the creditor nations may reap some benefit from capital flight, in the form of unrequited resource inflows that may offset deficits in other areas of the balance of payments of these countries, the beneficiaries of this process are generally not the same groups that bear the costs of debt renegotiations.

The hypothesis that incorrect data about foreign trade may be significantly impairing the ability of policy makers to manage the economy is supported by numerous recent analyses of international trade in Latin America. A revised foreign trade account based on accurate reporting of foreign trade and capital flows would indicate that many developing countries actually generate substantially more internal savings and suffer from a significantly less unfavorable balance of payments than is generally assumed based on the country's own statistics. The practical problem of inadequate internal savings and exports, then, is not simply the result of imbalances in the productive structure; it is likewise the product of capital flight, with the resulting gains to individual and corporate investors and losses to the country as a whole. Thus, a different view of foreign exchange availability based on a revision of the current account of the balance of payments might be the foundation for formulating a policy package that is more responsive to the country's needs.

Falsifying Invoices as a Mechanism for Capital Flight and Tax Evasion

As evidenced by the literature cited above, there is an increasing awareness that an important part of international capital movements is not reflected in existing balance-of-payments statistics. There are four important ways in which merchandise can be transferred between countries without being correctly documented: (1) the underinvoicing of exports, which permits foreign exchange earned abroad to remain abroad; (2) the overinvoicing of imports, to extract from a country a greater amount of foreign exchange than is required for the purchase of the goods actually imported (frequently this foreign exchange is obtained at preferential rates from governmental authorities); (3) the undeclared export or import of goods or services (including the underinvoicing of imports), to evade tax regulations or monetary controls; and (4) the use of "transfer pricing" among subsidiaries of a single firm, as part of a global strategy to minimize taxes and evade exchange controls by shifting profits to countries where taxes and controls are less onerous.

The fourth mechanism mentioned above is relatively well understood, although its quantitative importance is still difficult to determine (Kopits 1976). It permits the international transfer of profits but cannot be detected by comparing partner trading data. The third mechanism is commonly known as smuggling. Although less frequently discussed, the underinvoicing of imports, either in value or volume terms, provides a means for evading tariffs or other taxes but can only function when foreign exchange is available from free or parallel markets; international trade in drugs is included in the third mechanism.[4] The remaining two mechanisms, the underinvoicing of exports and overinvoicing of imports, are included in the professional literature as variants of the broader theme of smuggling. Widely practiced in weaker economies, they provide a means for evading income and profit taxes, import tariffs, and exchange controls, while also facilitating the obtainment of credits at preferential interest rates (for necessary imports or for bridge financing of exports).[5]

Circumventing international trade and currency regulations in the poorer countries most frequently involves a joint collaboration between people in the developing world and their trading partners abroad, as arrangements must be made to manage these funds and to divide the profits from such agreements. Increasingly, detailed studies have shown the way in which these processes operate in different markets and with various kinds of products (Bhagwati 1974; Walter 1987).

The Misreporting of Trade

As the falsified invoices discussed above are the basis for the reported statistics on trade, the consequence of these practices is the misreporting of trade. To examine the problem of capital flight related to the misreporting of merchandise trade, most studies compare aggregate export and income data among trading partners (Yeats 1978). When making such comparisons, discrepancies in the information on the value or the volume of trade can be attributed to a wide variety of factors.[6] Therefore, the simple identification of smuggling through aggregate statistical discrepancies in foreign trade data among trading partners misrepresents the nature of the problem. However, even without making the required adjustments to render trading partner data comparable, the discrepancies among countries are apparent. If the problem of underinvoicing in a number of developing economies is examined, it becomes manifest that the occurrence is greatest in those countries with the most serious macroeconomic adjustment problems (Table 4.1).[7]

In Latin America, there was underinvoicing of both exports and imports. Underinvoicing of imports is calculated to evade tariffs, which are high enough overall to outweigh capital flight as a motivation for the decision of how to invoice. Rudiger Dornbusch (1987) summarized the situation for Latin America cogently: "Export underinvoicing finances the tariff evasion by supplying the black market dollars required when import value is understated. It is striking and depressing that a whole continent's tax fraud should be so simple to document."

The large values for Mexico are characteristic of some of the countries that suffer from the greatest problem. A table of *unadjusted* differences in Mexico's trade with its principal trading partners reveals a widespread pattern of underinvoicing over the period from 1970 to 1985 (Table 4.2).[8]

TABLE 4.1
Underinvoicing of Foreign Trade, 1979–1985 (trade data ratios)

	EXPORTS								IMPORTS							
	1979	1980	1981	1982	1983	1984	1985	Average	1979	1980	1981	1982	1983	1984	1985	Average
All developing countries	11.6	10.7	13.9	16.4	10.9	11.1	12.3	12.4	2.9	1.6	-1.5	-3.4	-3.4	-2.5	5.9	-1.8
Africa	19.8	13.4	24.0	26.6	15.7	15.5	15.2	18.3	-1.8	-0.5	-8.7	-8.2	-6.9	-6.7	-8.6	-5.9
Asia	9.6	11.2	10.9	6.2	4.3	4.9	7.2	7.6	-5.2	-5.2	-9.2	-9.6	-10.6	-10.9	-11.8	-9.2
WesHem	16.2	17.6	18.3	19.3	18.5	17.3	18.5	18.0	10.8	7.8	7.1	9.8	16.0	21.7	6.2	10.6
Argentina	19.0	17.5	19.3	21.2	21.3	21.9	11.7	18.7	33.7	8.9	-1.3	2.6	26.4	17.0	-8.0	10.5
Brazil	17.3	14.7	11.6	16.1	9.9	11.7	21.8	14.7	-7.5	-8.8	-7.3	-0.8	-3.2	9.0	-1.8	-4.0
Chile	15.0	14.0	9.8	12.4	6.6	12.8	9.6	11.4	-7.8	-2.5	-8.3	2.1	4.1	11.6	1.5	-1.5
India	19.8	26.3	71.5	10.0	10.0	10.0	10.0	18.5	3.8	-1.3	24.7	-9.1	-9.1	-9.1	-9.1	-2.9
Korea	-0.4	0.7	-3.2	-5.8	-8.3	-7.9	2.2	-4.3	-10.1	-8.9	-17.2	-11.7	-9.7	-14.2	-11.4	-12.0
Mexico	42.6	27.8	27.3	27.5	27.8	22.2	25.8	27.3	29.0	30.6	23.8	31.7	65.8	59.6	14.3	32.2
Nigeria	15.5	10.0	27.8	27.0	10.0	10.0	10.0	15.5	-20.1	-9.1	-19.4	-19.3	-9.1	-9.1	-9.1	-14.9
Pakistan	13.5	14.6	8.1	14.5	.3	1.1	10.8	9.4	6.7	2.1	-3.2	4.8	10.5	15.0	8.2	6.5
Peru	9.0	14.6	18.2	10.0	10.0	10.0	10.0	11.7	43.8	33.9	23.1	-11.5	-11.5	-11.3	-11.5	15.6
Turkey	25.2	12.4	-1.3	-1.5	-4.9	-17.0	10.0	0.6	4.0	7.0	-3.9	-5.8	-3.1	-0.6	-9.1	-2.7
Uruguay	14.0	14.3	19.7	64.4	88.6	140.9	10.1	43.5	16.6	15.0	0.2	12.5	38.2	15.0	-9.2	10.7
Venezuela	1.7	5.4	10.7	10.0	10.0	10.0	10.0	8.3	-12.6	-17.6	-14.8	-9.9	-9.9	-9.9	-9.9	-12.6

Note: Figures refer to developing country exports to or imports from industrial countries. Trade data ratio is the difference between the developing country data, C, and the sum of the industrial countries data, P, divided by the developing country data: $(C-P) \div C$.

Source: IMF (International Monetary Fund), Directions of Trade Yearbook 1986, Washington, DC: IMF, 1986.

TABLE 4.2
Estimated Misreporting of Mexico's Trade (millions of U.S. dollars)

	1970	1971	1972	1973	1974	1975	1976	1977	1978	1979	1980	1981	1982	1983	1984	1985	Average
United States																	
Exports																	
U.S.A.	1,299	1,339	1,728	2,442	3,610	3,112	3,655	4,769	6,195	8,997	12,835	14,013	15,770	17,019	18,267	19,392	134,442
Mexico	839	911	1,288	1,318	1,703	1,668	2,111	2,738	4,057	6,252	10,072	10,716	11,129	13,034	14,612	15,029	97,477
Imports																	
U.S.A.	1,704	1,620	1,982	2,937	4,855	5,141	4,990	4,821	6,680	9,858	15,146	17,789	11,817	9,082	11,992	13,635	124,049
Mexico	1,568	1,479	1,775	2,277	3,779	4,113	3,773	3,493	4,564	7,563	11,979	15,398	9,006	4,958	6,695	11,132	93,552
Difference	596	569	647	1,784	2,983	2,472	2,761	3,359	4,254	5,040	5,930	5,688	7,452	8,109	8,952	6,866	67,462
% over	24.8	23.8	21.1	49.6	54.4	42.8	46.9	53.9	49.3	36.5	26.9	21.8	37.0	45.1	42.0	26.2	35.3
European Economic Community (ten members)																	
Exports																	
E.E.C.	139	134	149	218	416	388	421	499	501	630	1,448	2,120	2,360	2,447	2,590	2,409	16,869
Mexico	82	70	106	166	355	259	299	271	343	522	1,134	1,644	2,591	2,274	2,610	2,204	14,930
Imports																	
E.E.C.	484	502	558	772	1,117	1,204	1,085	915	1,634	2,128	3,025	3,541	2,438	1,572	1,548	1,849	2,4372
Mexico	462	466	576	645	1,065	1,091	984	809	1,398	1,955	2,557	3,029	2,224	1,082	1,232	1,625	2,1200
Difference	79	100	61	179	113	242	223	334	394	281	782	988	445	663	336	429	5,649
% over	14.5	18.7	8.9	22.1	8.0	17.9	17.4	30.9	22.6	11.3	21.2	21.1	9.2	19.8	8.7	11.2	15.6
Japan																	
Exports																	
Japan	151	170	202	276	308	212	249	304	358	479	939	1,435	1,520	1,890	2,255	1,884	12,632
Mexico	68	64	111	147	142	109	177	129	200	248	671	1,157	1,450	1,512	1,868	1,633	9,686
Imports																	
Japan	94	102	151	191	305	348	387	455	644	835	1,228	1,699	974	579	886	1,004	9,882
Mexico	86	90	115	178	224	299	307	296	609	790	989	1,205	855	320	457	914	7,734
Difference	91	118	127	142	247	152	152	334	193	276	507	772	189	637	816	341	5,094
% over	59.1	76.6	56.2	43.7	67.5	37.3	31.4	78.6	23.9	26.6	30.5	32.7	8.2	34.8	35.1	13.4	29.2

	1970	1971	1972	1973	1974	1975	1976	1977	1978	1979	1980	1981	1982	1983	1984	1985	Average
Spain																	
Exports																	
Spain	22	17	26	33	60	38	34	60	123	419	1,272	1,988	1,856	1,877	1,721	1,726	11,272
Mexico	14	10	16	33	47	20	20	62	153	458	1,238	1,921	1,815	1,617	1,703	1,590	10,717
Imports																	
Spain	29	45	62	56	61	60	62	67	111	251	417	534	526	258	207	245	2,991
Mexico	30	40	59	60	72	58	50	87	95	223	348	472	370	152	179	224	2,519
Difference	9	12	13	4	24	20	26	22	46	67	103	129	197	366	46	157	1,241
% over	20.5	24.0	17.3	4.3	20.2	25.6	37.1	14.8	18.5	9.8	6.5	5.4	9.0	20.7	2.4	8.7	9.4
Canada																	
Exports																	
Canada	45	50	53	83	117	93	148	184	162	178	295	797	806	875	1,110	976	5,972
Mexico	12	18	21	30	64	43	48	45	62	75	117	661	584	467	495	614	3,356
Imports																	
Canada	91	80	101	120	185	218	219	206	203	207	419	609	369	310	278	287	3,902
Mexico	49	48	75	85	146	146	141	166	126	198	353	446	320	206	207	256	2,968
Difference	75	64	58	88	92	122	178	179	177	112	244	299	271	512	686	393	3,550
% over	123.0	97.0	60.4	76.5	43.8	64.6	94.2	84.8	94.1	41.0	51.9	27.0	30.0	76.1	97.7	45.2	56.1
World Total																	
Difference	850	863	906	2,197	3,459	3,008	3,340	4,228	5,064	57,76	7,566	7,876	8,554	10,287	10,836	8,186	5,187

Source: IMF (International Monetary Fund), *Directions of Trade Yearbook, 1976, 1980, 1986*, Washington, DC: IMF, 1976, 1980, 1986.

The table reveals a systematic pattern of both underinvoicing of exports and underinvoicing of imports; in both cases the differences are greater than could be explained by the discrepancies mentioned above. The import picture is particularly noteworthy, as one would normally expect the Mexican figures to be higher than the trading partner data because of the cost of transport and insurance; thus, the discrepancies on the import side must, in reality, be even larger. The increase in the mid-1970s and the even larger jump in 1983 likely reflect a private reaction to official attempts to impose systems of foreign exchange controls that were particularly easy to evade with underinvoicing. Figure 4.1a shows the evolution of underinvoicing in Mexico's trade with the world, and Figure 4.1b details the phenomenon with the industrial countries during the first half of the 1980s.

To examine the significance of misreporting of merchandise trade in greater detail, and to circumvent the methodological limitations of this global approach, a different methodology was developed.[9] This approach goes beyond the more generally used aggregate analysis to identify individual products that might have been favored as vehicles for the international transfer of funds. Unit prices derived from data for tradeable commodities in Mexican fruit and vegetable markets were used to evaluate the extent of under- or overinvoicing. This unit price comparison, covering a four-year period, including a two-year base period in which the under- or over-reporting was assumed not to have been a problem, identified more than six hundred commodities for which prices had changed dramatically (Barkin 1984). Some of these products were examined in greater detail to determine the possibility of misleading or erroneous information in the foreign trade accounts. One example, relating to tomatoes, is sufficient to illustrate the procedure.

Unit prices of tomato exports were compared over the period from 1980 to 1983. The average for the 1980–1981 period was used as the base period to predict the expected value of exports for 1982 and 1983. Results for 1982 were excluded because of the peculiar economic climate prevailing in Mexico in that year; the adjusted results suggest unreported export earnings in 1983 of $112 million for this one commodity (Table 4.3).

To further examine the problem and test the above procedure, an alternative method, based on comparing trading partner statistics at the commodity level, was used (Table 4.4). U.S. data on imports from Mexico and Mexican records on exports to the United States were compared. These sources confirmed the existence of substantial underinvoicing of tomato exports from Mexico to the United States in 1983, when the two countries reported approximately the same trade volume. The reported

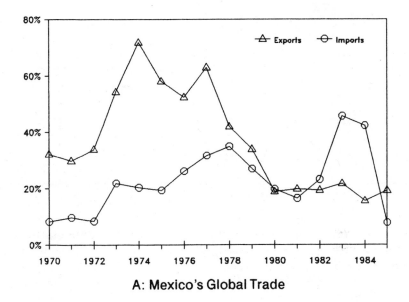

A: Mexico's Global Trade

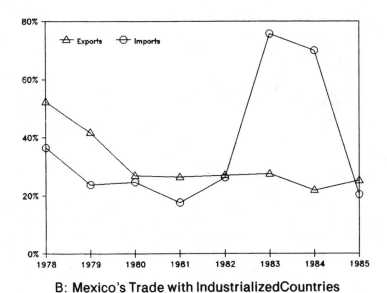

B: Mexico's Trade with IndustrializedCountries

FIGURE 4.1 Misreporting of Mexican Trade

Source: IMF (International Monetary Fund), *Directions of Trade Yearbook 1976, 1980, 1986,* Washington, DC: IMF, 1976, 1980, 1986.

TABLE 4.3
Determination of Underinvoicing,
Unit Pricing Methodology (tomatoes)

Year	Unit Prices	Export Volume	Reported Values	Predicted Values[a]	Estimated Underinvoicing[a]
1980	.446	373	166	[b]	0[b]
1981	.854	293	250	[b]	0[b]
1982	.266	579	154	376	222
1983	.325	344	112	224	112

[a]Millions of U.S. dollars.
[b]Base year.

Sources: IMCE (Instituto Mexicano de Comercio Exterior), foreign trade data (computer data bank); SPP (Secretaría de Programación y Presupuesto), INEGI (Instituto Nacional de Estadística, Geografía e Informática), *Anuario Estadístico de Comercio Exterior*, Mexico City: SPP, INEGI, various years.

amount of underinvoicing is virtually the same for 1983 with the two methods: more than 100 percent of the value declared in Mexico.[10]

By applying this same method of comparing trading partner statistics to the sale of Mexican bananas in the United States, the analysis revealed a 142 percent underinvoicing of exports from Mexico in 1983, a result that was not detectable by the unit price procedure because the international price of bananas rose in the years following the base period.

These statistical studies were complemented by interviews with people directly involved in the export of fruits and vegetables from Mexico and with the brokers in the United States. The interviewers were able to confirm the high degree of collaboration between the U.S. buyers and the Mexican sellers. Well-compensated intermediaries facilitated the process by arranging for international bank transfers and new accounts, co-signing as guarantors, and providing financial intermediation services to ensure that the "extra" funds were safely deposited according to the instructions of the exporter. Though most of the differences were the result of underinvoicing of exports, the researchers discovered that some of the discrepancies were the result of misreporting by the U.S. brokers who were also transferring profits to other countries or other lines of business to evade taxation.

Subsequent investigation in other industries revealed that the process is widespread among a broad spectrum of entrepreneurs engaged in both the export and import of commodities. Four industrial sectors that

TABLE 4.4
Determination of Underinvoicing,
Comparison of Trading Partner Data

	1982	1983
Tomatoes		
Value		
Exports (Mexico source)	153.8	111.8
Imports (U.S. source)	173.4	226.8
Underinvoicing	19.6	115.0
% Underinvoicing		102.9
Volume		
Exports (Mexico source)	338.2	206.2
Imports (U.S. source)	267.2	331.7
Bananas		
Value		
Exports (Mexico source)	1.422	3.775
Imports (U.S. source)	3.050	9.120
Underinvoicing	1.628	5.345
% Underinvoicing		141.6
Volume		
Exports (Mexico source)	7.0	30.7
Imports (U.S. source)	11.4	36.9

Note: Values are millions of U.S. dollars, volumes are in metric tons.

Source: IMCE (Instituto Mexicano de Comercio Exterior), foreign trade data (computer data bank).

merit particularly detailed investigation are chemicals; base metals and derived products; machinery and equipment, including electrical goods; and transport equipment. As the researchers probed deeper into the issue, they also found small but significant differences in unit prices for raw materials entering into international trade from both private and public agencies on both sides of the border. These extra funds were apparently used to pay various forms of commissions to participants in the transactions.

The field research and quantitative analysis demonstrate that during economic crises the use of the various forms of smuggling as mechanisms

TABLE 4.5
Index of Overinvoicing Imports[a]

	All Imports Trade Data Ratio (1)	Apparent Overinvoicing Number of Cases (2)	Apparent Overinvoicing Trade Data Ratio (3)	Index of Overinvoicing (3÷1)
Ecuador	0.82	37	1.52	1.85
Guatemala	0.99	34	1.98	2.00
Venezuela	1.07	71	1.44	1.35

[a]The index of overinvoicing is a comparison of the trade data ratios of the selected group of commodities to the total trade between the countries and the United States.

Note: The cases refer to four- and five-digit SITC categories.

Source: United Nations, *Commodity Trade Statistics* (computer data bank), based on data in David Barkin, "La Sobrefacturación de las Importaciones: Un Estudio Empírico," *Economía: Teoría y Práctica*, No. 14, 1990, p. 11.

of capital flight is shockingly pervasive. Preliminary estimates based on an analysis of the trade data for 1983 suggest that the detectable over- and underinvoicing of Mexico's foreign trade in that critical year might have been several billion dollars.[11]

A parallel investigation of the overinvoicing of exports from the United States to Guatemala, Ecuador, and Venezuela yielded analogous findings. If trading partner data at the five-digit SITC (standard international trade classification) level of disaggregation were used, a systematic pattern of overinvoicing in some commodities could be differentiated from an overall picture of apparent neutrality. The majority of the trade categories and the most valuable import items that were readily identified as probable cases of overinvoicing were concentrated in the chemicals and basic manufacturing sectors (SITC 5 and 6). The value of the imported commodities so identified amounted to 16 percent of total imports in Ecuador, 15 percent in Guatemala, and 9 percent in Venezuela. This over-reporting, measured by the trade data ratio, amounted to a combined total of 52 percent for thirty-seven SITC categories in Ecuador, 98 percent for thirty-four cases in Guatemala, and 44 percent for seventy-one groupings in Venezuela (Table 4.5). The overall index of overinvoicing[12] was 1.85 for Ecuador, 2.0 for Guatemala, and 1.35 for Venezuela, indicating that for the selected group of commodities where overinvoicing was observed the discrepancies were substantially greater than the overall discrepancies for all exports from the United States to the three countries.

Smuggling and Development Finance

In this chapter I suggest that the Mexican economy generated substantially more foreign exchange and savings than could be reported. This implies that *the traditional definition of the development problem is seriously deficient* and that the perceived shortage of foreign exchange and internal savings that is generally identified as the heart of the development problem is at best a symptom of the greater problem of social conflict, which is manifest in capital flight. By examining the misreporting of foreign trade, it is distressingly easy to substantiate the capital outflow phenomenon in a large number of countries. A close relationship between capital outflows and the increment in foreign debt is also evident.[13] Thus, it appears that private capital flight has been financed by the increase of public foreign debt.

The misreporting of trade flows—smuggling—which constitutes an important vehicle for capital flight, has serious welfare implications for the various countries involved. On balance, the over- and underinvoicing of trade is the equivalent of a decline in export prices and a rise in import costs: a deterioration in the terms of trade, but with the specific difference that the exporters, instead of bearing part of the burden along with the country as a whole, are the beneficiaries. In many developing countries, where trade taxes represent a significant part of total revenues,[14] this form of capital flight has a major impact on government finances: It erodes government revenues, forcing tax increases and cutbacks in development programs, and it restricts foreign exchange availability, requiring further currency depreciation, which in turn may induce increased capital outflows.[15] Heightened inflationary pressures and accelerated erosion of living standards are unavoidable consequences of capital flight.

In addition to these global effects, which seriously distort policy makers' understanding of the economy, there is the differential sectoral incidence of smuggling. Because the incorrectly valued goods are distributed unequally throughout the economy, a distorted picture of the relative productivity of the various sectors results in erroneous estimates of the productive potential of the different parts of the economy, with adverse consequences for global planning and growth. Finally, in periods of crisis, when capital flight increases, the lack of information about the magnitude and impact of the misreporting of trade flows probably leads to an underestimate of the relative decline in consumption by reducing the *apparent* fluctuations in imports and production for export. Thus, the withdrawal of funds from the country leaves policy makers ill prepared to anticipate some of the productive dislocations that may be affecting aggregate growth.

The developing countries with weak currencies are not the only casualties of this capital flight. Although the United States has been a major recipient of deposits as a result of flight, the adjustment difficulties in the debtor countries are occasioning serious economic disruption and financial management problems because of the burdens of capital flight and the threat of unilateral moratoria.[16] Now, there is clearly a global interest in international cooperation to stem capital flight.

The current-account discrepancy discussed in this chapter is the statistical manifestation of an assault by small groups of wealthy individuals on countries with weak currencies. These individuals are using the foreign trade process as well as other vehicles to enrich themselves at the expense of other social groups. In the process, they distort basic information in ways that impair their governments' capacity to manage the economy. Capital flight (including the non-repatriation of export earnings and income from investments held abroad) is a product of the individual search for greater financial security. Furthermore, "the net capital outflows . . . indicate that the IMF type retrenchment and restructuring policies . . . failed in most cases to staunch the outflow of capital" (Felix and Sánchez 1987). In fact, the accumulation of foreign assets by nationals of several countries with the heaviest debt burdens now exceeds the foreign debts of their home countries.[17] In this light, the task of economic policy making is not simply a problem of imposing controls on capital: Such controls rarely have proven effective. And administrative measures, such as the monitoring of trade flows, may provide limited relief, but cannot attack the heart of the problem. Likewise, neither exchange rate and interest rate adjustments nor programs to assure adequate volumes of investment or foreign exchange measure up to the challenge. Rather, the job at hand is to rebuild the productive base of the economy by reincorporating the masses of workers into production to create profitable investment opportunities in an expansive economic environment.

Notes

1. The estimates of capital outflow are subject to an important methodological dispute among the participating international organizations and scholars. The data presented here are taken from Pastor's analysis (1988) of Latin American capital flight. In many ways this analysis is similar to Dooley et al. (1986) and to a different approach taken by Ros (1986). Although the numbers differ, the

orders of magnitude are similar, and the conclusions I draw in the text would not be modified by accepting the estimates of a different source.

2. For an evaluation of this view of policy making in Mexico and an alternative explanation of the internal dynamics see Barkin and Esteva (1986).

3. One particularly devastating productive change has been the erosion of the ability of many developing countries to supply themselves with their own basic food needs in spite of the existence of idle natural and human resources that could be mobilized for such production. See Chapter 2 of this book and Barkin, Batt, and DeWalt (1990) for a global extension of the analysis.

4. Gulati (1987) suggests that the underinvoicing of imports to avoid tariff and tax payments may, in fact, be just as important or even more important than capital flight as a problem for developing countries. My analysis of his Mexican data on a commodity-by-commodity basis suggests that his findings may represent definitional differences in trading partner data (discussed in the text and in note 6, below) rather than the misreporting that leads to countervailing capital flows as he suggests.

Drug traffic probably also involves a substantial inflow of foreign exchange, which counterbalances the capital flight discussed in the present chapter. No reliable estimates of the magnitude of the value of this trade are available.

5. These practices—underinvoicing of exports and overinvoicing of imports— have been increasingly commented upon by the international academic and financial community as more global quantitative studies have documented the pervasiveness of the phenomenon (Bhagwati 1978; Cuddington 1986; Dornbusch 1987; Gulati 1987; Barkin 1989a). Unfortunately, most of the aggregate studies used to analyze falsified foreign trade invoices, including the materials cited here, use global data to measure the extent of the problem. For example, in a detailed aggregate study of Mexican trade with the United States, Carriles Rubio (1979) reduced the $6 billion and $2.968 billion discrepancies for 1975 and 1976 by adjusting for labor-intensive manufacturing assembly operations, precious metals, and the status of Puerto Rico; as a result, the differences were only about $85 million and $324 million, respectively. My calculations, however, suggest that such a sanguine evaluation is unwarranted, as compensating errors in both directions, undetected by Carriles's approach, tended to minimize the problem. During the period he considered, a selective examination of individual products indicated that some people were taking foreign exchange out of the country, perhaps as a response to the rising level of anxiety about economic management, while others were bringing capital into the country, perhaps as a response to the growing undervaluation of the peso, or were simply underinvoicing imports to avoid high tariff barriers.

6. These factors include differences in reporting periods, losses during transport and handling, and different definitions for recording. There are also differences attributable to technical problems: Exports are generally valued in FOB terms, while imports are reported in CIF values; in other cases, the valuation by one of the partners may be based on official internal prices rather than real transaction costs. The comparative exercise is further complicated by conceptual differences in the form in which the statistical data are collected (Veil [1982] presents a useful review of these problems).

The formal discrepancies are particularly great in the case of Mexico. There, following International Monetary Fund (IMF) guidelines, temporary imports by labor-intensive manufacturing assembly plants are not registered while exports include only the value added from the production process. In contrast, the United States includes in its trade data the full value of exports to and imports from these manufacturing plants. Similar differences exist with respect to silver and gold exports, which are treated as monetary transfers in Mexico but as merchandise elsewhere. Mexico considers Puerto Rico as a separate country in its foreign trade accounts, while the United States integrates this trade into its overall domestic accounts. The Bank of Mexico (Carriles Rubio 1979) shows that these corrections would substantially change the figures with respect to the United States; they might also introduce important changes in the comparisons with other trading partners because much of Mexico's trade goes through other countries (triangulation). (See McDonald [1985] for additional comments on this problem in reference to a number of other countries.) These discrepancies render incomplete such unadjusted comparisons as those reported in Table 4.2.

7. Because many of the countries shown in this table did not report their trade for recent years, the IMF used partner trading data or extrapolated on the basis of past experience. Therefore, on the export side the trade data ratios that approximate 10 are generally the product of this estimation procedure, which adds 10 percent for the costs of transport, insurance, etc.; on the import side the ratios of -9 to -11 are similarly the result of this estimation process.

8. To minimize problems of comparability, Table 4.2 is based on data from the IMF publication *Directions of Trade*, which reports country information from national sources. For Mexico, these data do not coincide with national statistics. Especially noteworthy is the recent change to an FOB basis in reporting Mexican import figures, beginning in 1983 (see, however, the comments in note 6 above). The export figures refer to Mexican exports and trading partner imports; import figures similarly refer to imports into Mexico and are compared with partner export figures. The differences are the sums of the absolute amounts of the export and import data.

9. This alternative method was developed in collaboration with Adriaan Ten Kate. The unit price method is most useful when examined in conjunction with an analysis of the evolution of world market prices for the commodities under scrutiny. It is important to note that both the unit price method and the comparison of trading partner data on the level of individual commodities (Table 4.4) can only be indicators of underinvoicing. Both approaches allow us to determine the existence of such practices and identify some vehicles for capital flight, but neither can be used to determine the size of the problem on a national level.

10. The comparisons among sources for tomatoes in Table 4.4 illustrate some of the pitfalls in attempting to systematize Mexican data. The data for this table are from the Instituto Mexicano de Comerico Exterior. In contrast, the official Mexican government *Statistical Yearbook* (published by INEGI, or Instituto Nacional de Estadística, Geografía, e Informática) reports an export volume of 578,725 tons (71 percent greater) for 1982 and 344,572 tons (67 percent higher) for 1983.

Using these numbers would affect the measure of underinvoicing, which was based on value terms, and the discrepancies among sources are significantly less.

11. Clearly, the Mexican authorities are becoming alarmed about the problem. In July 1984 the Mexican ministries of the Treasury and Commerce issued a joint communiqué to announce their intention to attempt to control the "disloyal practice" of over- and underinvoicing in foreign trade. They charged the Bank of Mexico with responsibility for overseeing and controlling the situation, and in 1986 a new foreign trade law introduced, among other things, a working group that specifically addresses itself to "disloyal practices." No practical results are yet observable as a result of these modifications.

12. The index of overinvoicing is a comparison of the trade data ratios of the selected group of commodities to the total trade between the countries and the United States.

13. The strong debt–capital outflow relationship has been established by a number of researchers using a variety of testing and modeling techniques (Khan and Ul Haque 1985; Cuddington 1986; Felix and Sánchez 1987).

14. The IMF reported that in 1982 trade taxes amounted to 15.5 percent of revenues in Africa, 19.1 percent in Asia, and 14.4 percent in Latin America; trade taxes were 2.9 percent, 3.2 percent, and 2.9 percent, respectively, of gross national product (GNP) in that year (IMF, *Government Finance Statistics Yearbook 1986*, pp. 48–49, 74–75).

15. Dornbusch (1987) and Pastor (1988) provide lengthy discussions of these macroeconomic effects.

16. The Chair of the U.S. International Trade Commission attributed a loss of 1 million manufacturing jobs in the United States to the Latin American debt crisis. The Joint Economic Committee (JEC) of the U.S. Congress blames part of the depth and duration of the farm depression on the same cause (JEC 1986, cited in Felix and Sánchez 1987).

17. Felix and Sánchez (1987), using IMF and Federal Reserve Bank data, estimate the ratio of foreign assets to foreign debt for 1985 to be 1.08 each for Argentina and Mexico and 2.42 for Venezuela. The ratio was .34 for Brazil, up from .17 in 1977; .2 for Peru; and −.16 for Chile.

5

The Limits of Capitalist Development

Mexico's economic development proceeded for decades on the assumption that the benefits from a rising national product and progressive industrialization would eventually trickle down to the masses. Although capitalist accumulation programs have never been based on illusions about their objectives—increasing profits by broadening markets through employing more workers—the Mexican state rarely could dedicate itself single-mindedly to pursue these objectives; popular mobilizations of workers and small farmers have repeatedly exacted concessions from the government to improve social services and raise wages. Most government programs, however, are oriented to stimulating economic growth by providing the infrastructure necessary to spark private investment and create an environment conducive to profit making. But the very success of the government's pro-business policies has depended on the state's great flexibility in responding, when necessary, to urban and rural demands to share in economic growth through increases in wages or benefits.

Until recently, the outstanding characteristic of modern Mexican economic development has been its ability to incorporate virtually the entire population and productive structure into a market economy. Since 1940, the shift away from an agrarian society and the sweeping emphasis on industrialization have wrought profound changes in the type of goods available, and the new systems for producing these goods have made it impossible for any group of Mexican society to escape the influence of the market in daily life. Even rural communities that have been able to preserve cooperative forms of production find that their decisions about how and what to produce are affected definitively by national and international market forces beyond their control and, often, even unknown to them. The reemergence of a polarized agricultural structure is the result of official decisions to accede to international pressures to encourage commercial agricultural production, both for wealthy consumers in Mexico and for export, at the expense of basic food production by the majority of the country's small-scale farmers. The same is true for consumption patterns, which also have been radically altered by changing lifestyles, migration, labor force demands, and social structures. These transformations, in turn, can be traced to the profound modifications in the productive apparatus occasioned by Mexico's progressive entrance into the world economy (described in the first chapter of this book).

The reorientation of the economy toward industrial production has penalized the vast majority of direct producers, who have not been able to participate in the new growth sectors. The economic system is no longer able to supply the foodstuffs and other basic commodities required by the majority of Mexicans for their very survival. Food, housing, medical care, and education are among the critical products in short supply. Modernization of the economy has created a small industrial proletariat and expanded many middle sectors including intellectuals, bureaucrats, professionals, and technicians. Mexico's economy can now produce a wide range of consumer durables and basic inputs needed for producing these consumer goods, which gives it the façade of a modern, industrializing power. But to sustain this activity Mexico must import its capital goods (machinery and equipment) along with many intermediate goods required for production as well as components and spare parts. Local technological development has been virtually non-existent while consumption patterns have become increasingly internationalized. For many Mexicans, development itself seems irrelevant.

In this chapter, I present a broad outline of Mexico's development process. I briefly trace the nature of the process that distributed benefits unequally among the various competing social groups in the first section. In the second section, I examine capitalist development in Mexico in the light of the evolution of the world economy as a whole. The third section contains an analysis of the structural transformations in production along with some consideration of who were the principal actors. Finally, I evaluate the internal and external contradictions that arose as a result of decades of capitalist accumulation and created the profound crisis in which the country finds itself at present.

The Beneficiaries of Capitalist Development

One of the most remarkable aspects of Mexico's history of structural transformation is the accompanying widespread improvement in social welfare. Beginning in the 1940s and continuing into the early 1970s, real standards of living continued to improve, slowed only by a decline in the rate of growth of gross domestic product (GDP) during the late

1960s. Even in the rural sector, real incomes climbed steadily as productivity rose in dryland agriculture and new crops were introduced in irrigated areas. Employment opportunities increased as industry, commercial agriculture, and public investment expanded. Though worker and farmer incomes were rising, a substantial change in the social composition of the population was taking place: self-employed urban and rural workers were transformed into wage-laborers or piece-rate workers throughout the society. The growth of the bureaucracy went unchecked until recently, expanding more than tenfold since 1940 to a high of more than 2 million positions in the 1980s.

Government policies took up where the marketplace left off, fostering further improvements in living standards. From 1940 to 1975, there were continuing efforts to expand the public educational system and improve the quality and volume of medical services available to the population. Although the public schools and universities still function as a mechanism for stratifying and channeling people by social class into different occupational categories (Barkin 1975), the ebullient growth of the period opened opportunities for many, who were able to escape from their "tracks" and find paths to upward social and economic mobility. The growth of a university system, which now has more than 700,000 students, spawned the emergence of important new professional groups who adopted the lifestyles and consumption patterns offered by the panoply of consumer-oriented industries. At the same time, improvements in public health lowered mortality rates, especially among infants, and raised life expectancy, while nutritional levels slowly improved. In spite of this, large segments of the population were living in poverty with their basic needs unmet. Even before the current crisis, the widespread prevalence of malnutrition, illiteracy, and serious health problems was broadly acknowledged (Lustig 1987).

Mexico's capitalist development also created a highly favorable environment for private domestic investors. Protective tariff barriers, permissive domestic legislation, and regressive taxation policies facilitated the growth of consumer goods industries, which thrived in the hothouse of rapidly expanding internal demand from the burgeoning middle and upper classes. Consequently, local markets were dynamic, and competition was sufficiently limited to create the possibility of windfall profits for industrial producers throughout the economy.

The prosperity generated by high rates of economic growth and the broadening of the market stimulated by a substantial program of government investments altered the structure of ownership and control of the Mexican economy. Throughout the society, large enterprises consolidated and absorbed or destroyed medium-sized firms, while small farms and workshops stagnated. In rural Mexico, the smallholder sector declined while better capitalized, larger scale, commercial farmers and ranchers took advantage of export opportunities and supplied expanding demand from the middle sectors and from industries requiring animal feeds. Profits of successful firms were enhanced by government tax abatements and subsidy programs reducing energy costs and interest rates for new investments in equipment. This same process of concentration and centralization also polarized the industrial sector, leading to the destruction of many medium-sized producers as large conglomerates thrived in the protected environment that allowed them to grow rapidly, while most very small workshops (with from one to five people) continued to proliferate in marginal circumstances (Trejo Reyes 1983). Among financial firms, too, control grew increasingly centralized as powerful banks acquired numerous enterprises, gaining control over the nation's most important industries; a small group of very powerful private financiers managed the country's financial resources and determined the economic fortunes of many businesses. These financiers engaged in a bitter struggle with the government over the direction in which the economy should evolve and in the process rapidly assumed control of important parts of the leading industrial and commercial conglomerates during the decade prior to the nationalization of the banking system in 1982 (Cordera and Tello 1983).

The accelerating concentration of control over the productive apparatus has been far more important than rising income levels in determining the overall welfare impact of economic development in Mexico. In the ultimate analysis, as events in the 1980s have shown, increases in monetary income can be eroded rapidly by an incomes policy that systematically redistributes benefits toward the middle groups through wage and employment policies (Table 5.1a). This is exactly what has happened in Mexico: In spite of decades of rapid growth of the labor force and real increases in the general standard of living, the recent economic crisis, dating from 1976, has progressively eroded years of gains by the country's working classes, reducing labor's share in GDP (Table 5.1b); this is examined in greater detail in the next chapter.

Since the 1960s, it has become fashionable in the social sciences to emphasize the heightening concentration of personal incomes during Mexico's period of rapid economic growth. Even after the implementation of relatively strong redistributive measures during the first half of the 1970s, Mexico was characterized by the World Bank as having "one of the worst profiles of income distribution of any nation on earth" (*World Development Report, 1980*, 1980, p. 50 and Figure 4.4). The income distribution data clearly illustrate the sharp deterioration in the share of personal income enjoyed by the poorest 40 percent of the population in the three decades following the Second World War (Table 5.1a). The

TABLE 5.1
Measures of Income Distribution

A. Distribution of Personal Income, 1950–1984 (percentages)

Income Group	1950	1963	1970	1977	1984
Lowest 20 percent	5.6	3.7	3.8	3.3	4.0
Second quintile	7.5	6.8	8.0	7.7	8.8
Third Quintile	10.9	11.2	13.7	12.9	14.2
Fourth quintile	16.7	20.2	18.7	21.1	22.4
Fifth quintile	59.3	58.1	55.8	55.0	50.6
(of which) Top 10%	45.5	41.6	39.2	38.0	33.5

B. Participation of Labor in Gross Domestic Product

	1940	1950	1960	1970	1980	1988
Share of labor	29.1	25.3	31.2	35.7	36.0	25.9

Sources: A) SARH (Secretaría de Agricultura y Recursos Hidráulicos), *Estadísticas Básicas 1960–1986 para la Planeación del Desarrollo Rural Integral*, Mexico City: SARH, 1986. B) Jeffery Bortz, ed., *La Estructura de Salarios en México*, Mexico City: Universidad Autónoma Metropolitana, Atzcapotzalco, 1985; SPP (Secretaría de Programación y Presupuesto), INEGI (Instituto Nacional de Estadística, Geográfia, e Informática), *Sistemas de Cuentas Nacionales de México, 1985–1988*, Mexico City: SPP, INEGI, 1990.

decline in the share going to the richest 10 percent of the population reflects a redistribution within the upper and middle sectors rather than a reversal of the overall trend toward concentration. The severe deterioration in the relative position of the lowest income group in 1977 is particularly noteworthy, because it comes after a period when government programs were supposed to have been populist and, therefore, redistributive. In addition, the 1977 figures fail to take into account the decline in the real purchasing power of salaries, which commenced in 1976 and continues through the end of the 1980s.[1] The skewing of the income distribution becomes far more striking if one considers the growing proportion of the labor force—more than one-half in the 1980s—that is working at salaries below the official minimum daily wage. This trend has intensified as the crisis deepened throughout the decade. (See

Figure 6.1 in Chapter 6 for a review of the purchasing power of minimum salaries.)

Thus, although capitalist development did initially stimulate a process of real improvements in living standards for all social groups, the economic crisis that began in 1976 reversed this trend for small farmers, salaried workers, and professionals. Even at the height of the period of prosperity, when workers and small farmers enjoyed important improvements in their real purchasing power and gained broader access to basic social services, the lion's share of the benefits from growth was consistently appropriated by capital. The concentration of personal income and the centralization of control over the productive apparatus was financed by the extraordinarily high profits generated in the overly protective environment carefully shaped by the state, which was particularly solicitous of the business class.

The Gestation of the Mexican Crisis

During four decades, Mexico, and most of its social groups, enjoyed a period of prosperity. The rising living standards, broadening middle sectors, and expansion and diversification of highly profitable entrepreneurial activities combined to create the "Mexican miracle," as it was enshrined in the literature. This notable aberration in the behavior of capitalist systems in the third world is worthy of analysis.

The Mexican miracle began with some measure of restraint during World War II (Niblo 1988). As part of Mexico's contribution to the war effort, the government imposed strict controls on domestic wages and reorganized production to supply the Allies with scarce goods; the alacrity of this effort drove the country to the brink of famine in 1944, as a result of the massive displacement of basic food crops for oil-bearing seeds. Because wages were tightly controlled, profits from war-related production and import substitution accumulated rapidly. During the immediate postwar years, 1948–1954, rapid increases in production were made possible by mobilizing underutilized domestic labor, natural resources, and accumulated international reserves. Later, internal political control carefully doled out limited improvements in living conditions to ever-widening segments of the population. Capitalists, too, were encouraged and even anxious to reinvest their earnings in a promising new market and did so, either individually or jointly, with foreign capital. The labor unrest of the late 1950s was widely dismissed (by political leaders) as the result of undisciplined greed by a few worker groups whose impatience might upset the process of orderly growth and redistribution.

Continued growth in the 1950s began to require compromises and restraint. Price stability could not be maintained without conflict if government expenditures rose along with profits. By 1965, the model of political negotiation that combined selective, efficient repression with measured doses of charity for the majority of workers and small farmers and unbridled generosity for investors required more resources than were available to either the government or the private sector.

Beginning in the 1960s, international events began to play an important role in Mexico's political economy. Mexico offered an attractive alternative model of economic development that could be a foil to the inspiring successes of the Cuban Revolution. The United States was heavily embroiled in an (eventually) losing struggle in Vietnam that provoked internal contradictions within U.S. society, making Mexican labor, although nominally illegal, vital for production in several regions of the United States. In this context, private investors and governments in the advanced capitalist nations responded favorably to Mexican requests for more resources by proffering grants and loans, which were aimed at defusing internal dissent occasioned by the intensifying problems of insufficient employment creation, inadequate public services, and insufficient government revenues. It later became evident that these offerings from the international community were not simply postponing but also aggravating some of the very problems that they were attempting to resolve.

With the advancement of Mexico's gradual integration into the world economy, the country faced new demands and pressures from external forces. The Mexican model, as it had evolved, was extremely inefficient and required growing subsidies and financial aid from abroad to sustain domestic production and finance governmental programs. International capital could not permit such undisciplined behavior indefinitely. Structural changes were needed to impose a greater measure of restraint on social actors, especially workers and small farmers, and to reorganize production so that Mexico could more readily transfer resources—raw materials, finished products, labor, and profits—to the international centers of capital accumulation. Real wages would have to decline, along with the prevailing standard of living, to free resources for this transfer and to cheapen Mexican labor so that international capital might set up new profit centers in the country.

The new Mexican development model, which evolved after 1976, dramatically changed the nature of the state as well as the country's role in the international economy. No longer could Mexico afford to be simply a showcase of third world capitalist development. The cost of doing so has always been beyond its means, and now the international community no longer is willing to continue financing the Mexican program. Instead, world bankers now demand that Mexico must become a full partner in world capitalist development, contributing with its resources, its products, and its labor power to the global process of centralizing economic power. As the Secretariat of the GATT (General Agreement on Tariffs and Trade) stated in its annual review of the international economy in 1982: "In an open economic system, one of the principal functions of trade policy is to guarantee the consistency of national economic policy among nations and on an international plane" (GATT, *International Trade Annual, 1982* [Geneva: Gatt, 1982]). Undoubtedly, this means the subordination of national objectives and needs to the imperatives of international accumulation. An alternative is possible, but it requires raising certain economic needs, such as food production, to the level of national priorities as a complement to the ongoing process of international integration.

Successful Capitalist Development

In the midst of an economic crisis it is sometimes difficult to appreciate the long history of capitalist success that ultimately drove Mexico to its present difficulties. A review of this history reveals first how successful this development was. Modern Mexico's highly diversified industrial and agricultural structure is the result of the remarkable consistency in overall economic and political goals of the presidential administrations during almost a half century since 1935.

Successive administrations have frequently changed the instruments to promote development and adapt to evolving conditions within the country and in the international economy. But the common commitment to integrate myriad ethnic groups into a coherent national identity while promoting private industrial development and developing a modern, market-oriented agricultural sector has been unwavering. Although the attitude is less apparent as a thread of continuity, the creation of a developed national economic structure has never been viewed in official circles as incompatible with a strong foreign presence, which first penetrated resource-based enclaves in mining and agriculture and then sped the development of an increasingly complex industrial structure. But foreign influence and control extends beyond a simple inventory of firms owned directly by non-Mexicans or controlled through local corporate or personal shells. The country's recent (1986) accession to the international free trade organization (the GATT), the substantial liberalization of foreign trade and investment policy, and the ongoing negotiations to restructure the foreign debt and its servicing are only the most recent manifestations of Mexico's integration into the world economy— an integration that has penetrated virtually every aspect of social, political, and economic life.

Several methods may be used to detect and describe the transformations that are causing permanent, sweeping changes throughout the Mexican economy. Traditionally, economists define structural changes in terms of the distribution of national product among the various types of economic activity (Table 5.2a). Thus, the substantial redistribution of national product from agriculture toward industry is generally considered sufficient evidence of significant modifications in Mexican production since 1940. Similarly, the important relative decline of the secondary sector in the 1980s provides eloquent testimony of the contraction of demand among middle sectors and the growing unemployment brought on by the crisis.

There are, however, even more revealing ways of examining the structural changes rocking the Mexican economy. The distribution of the labor force illustrates this process (Table 5.2b). The massive transfer of workers from the primary sector to the service (tertiary) sector reflects several related changes: (1) the decline in the share of the labor force in agriculture is a result of the sector's inability to absorb its traditionally large share of the new entrants into the labor force; (2) even during the period of rapid industrialization (1950–1970), the secondary sector was unable to absorb the majority of the people entering the labor force and relegated them to diverse activities in the tertiary sector; and (3) the service sector itself was changing as highly productive modern activities in some areas grew up alongside sales and personal services, which absorbed vast numbers of people whose productivity and income were low. More recently, however, the crisis of the 1980s has slowed the transfer from agriculture as the bottlenecks in labor recruitment in the rest of the economy make it difficult for small farmers and rural workers to simply abandon their farming communities in search of brighter horizons; although the prospects for work as migratory workers in the United States have improved with the amnesty program, most Mexican workers in the United States are still part of the Mexican labor force and frequently return to their communities of origin.

The analysis of productivity changes (Table 5.2c) also offers a clear indicator of economic restructuring. Labor productivity in the service sector has been declining relative to the other sectors since 1950 and absolutely in real terms since 1970 as workers have been forced into personal services and sales for lack of opportunities in the rest of the economy. Agricultural output per worker grew substantially in the 1960s, as part of the process of mechanization and irrigation development discussed in Chapter 2 of this book; rising agricultural productivity in the 1970s continues in spite of the crisis in the 1980s, providing striking evidence of the ability of a small group of commercial farmers to increase their export production. Despite the low levels of labor productivity

TABLE 5.2
Mexican Economic Structure and Growth, 1940–1988

Sector[a]	1940	1950	1960	1970	1980	1988	Annual Rates of Growth				
							1940-1950	1950-1960	1960-1970	1970-1980	1980-1988

A. Distribution of National Product (percent)

Total[b]	350	624	1,256	2,356	4,470	4,879	6.0	6.1	6.5	6.6	-1.9
Primary	19	19	16	11	8	8	5.8	4.2	3.0	3.4	-2.3
Secondary	25	27	26	31	33	32	6.6	7.1	7.9	7.4	-1.3
Tertiary	56	54	58	58	59	60	5.7	6.2	6.6	6.7	-2.2

B. Distribution of the Labor Force (percent)

Total[c]	5.86	8.27	11.33	12.96	20.28	21.8[d]	3.5	3.2	1.4	4.6	1.0
Primary	65	58	54	39	28	28	2.3	2.5	-1.8	1.1	0.8
Secondary	16	16	19	23	23	21	3.8	5.0	3.3	4.6	-0.2
Tertiary	19	26	27	38	49	51	4.7	5.3	3.4	9.2	1.7

C. Labor Productivity by Sector (national average = 100)

Total[e]	59.7	75.5	99.6	171.6	220	220[d]	2.4	2.8	5.6	2.5	-0.3
Primary	30	33	29	30	29	31	3.4	1.7	5.7	2.5	1.0
Secondary	197	166	154	150	143	145	0.7	2.0	5.3	2.0	0.8
Tertiary	291	253	210	169	120	118	0.9	0.9	3.3	-0.9	-0.5

[a]The sectors are defined as follows: primary–agriculture, livestock, forestry, and fishing; secondary–manufacturing, construction, mining petroleum, and electricity; tertiary–transportation, communications, commerce, finance, government, and other services.
[b]Millions of 1980 pesos.
[c]Millions of people.
[d]Data for 1987.
[e]Thousands of 1980 pesos.

Sources: SPP (Secretaría de Programación y Presupuesto), INEGI (Instituto Nacional de Estadística, Geográfia, e Informática), Sistema de Cuentas Nacionales de México, 1960–1985, 1981–1987, 1985–1988, Mexico City: SPP, INEGI, 1986, 1988, 1990; SPP, INEGI, Estadísticas Históricas de México, 2 vols., Mexico City: SPP, INEGI, 1985.

among other primary producers, these small farmers and rural workers have few more productive options elsewhere in Mexico.

The structural changes that led to the growing differences in productivity among sectors account for an important characteristic of Mexican development: *the extraordinary polarization of society in all its dimensions.* The enormous social and economic disparities among social classes, discussed in Chapter 2 and in the present chapter, reflect the sizable productivity differences among Mexican workers. These differences within each sector and across sectors are an important underlying cause of social stratification in Mexico. In agriculture, for example, microeconomic studies of smallholder communities demonstrate that the small farms using traditional cultivation methods are often significantly more efficient in using and combining their scarce resources, land, and capital than any other type of productive organization (Schultz 1964). In spite of this, small-farmer labor productivity is lower, because of smallholders' limited access to credit to purchase modern productive inputs.

Within the manufacturing sector productivity differences among firms are not only notable, but also, on average, substantially higher than in other sectors of the economy. These differences are highly correlated with the accelerated pace of centralization of control over enterprises that has been reshaping industry during recent decades (Hernández Laos 1983). Large integrated manufacturing firms are displacing or absorbing the smaller ones, with resulting modifications in the products that are available, the work process, and the groups that control the means of production. Production shifted to expand the availability of increasingly sophisticated and expensive upper income consumer goods, which are then purchased by lower income groups at the expense of basic goods essential for an adequate living standard. This pattern of consumer-durables production (e.g., household electronics) further divided society, concentrating economic power in highly capitalized industrial groups while splitting the labor force, affording jobs for a small group of highly trained workers and driving the mass of unskilled manual laborers into the informal sector. Traditional, labor-intensive enterprises fell victim to a distinct competitive disadvantage in the modernization process, beginning in the mid-1960s (Trejo Reyes 1971). The program of industrial reconversion, begun in the late 1970s, has led to an accelerating centralization of control of production and finance, along with the promotion of export-oriented firms in the industrial sector and a significant rise in labor productivity in industry. The convergence and concentration of financial and industrial interests in the same few hands became evident with the nationalization of the banking system in 1982 and the consequent separation of industrial conglomerates from the financial sector.[2]

In services, labor productivity actually began to fall even before the onset of the economic crisis, although it is still higher than in the rural areas. The un- and underemployed, who had nowhere else to go, have flocked into marginal activities in commerce and personal services, especially since the decision to discourage basic food production in the 1970s. In spite of substantial increases in the productivity of modern service industries, such as banking, communications, and transport, and the sweeping centralization of merchandising with the spread of shopping centers and supermarkets in the 1980s, itinerant merchants and readily available service workers have proliferated throughout the country. During the height of the government-induced prosperity of the late 1970s and the boom years of a fleeting petroleum-driven prosperity, there was a marked tightening of the labor market (i.e., a temporary shortage of labor). This changed with the heightening of crisis, and underemployment has expanded to become an increasingly worrisome social phenomenon. The tertiary sector continues to be a sink for the rejects from other sectors, the social outcasts that Mexico's modernizing capitalist economy is incapable of absorbing productively.

The Changing Composition of Output

The divergent trends in productivity growth also reflect the changing structure of commodities produced in Mexico. Not only have large, modern firms displaced traditional producers in both agriculture and industry, but they have also changed the country's physiognomy. In agriculture, production shifted from basic human foodstuffs to animal feeds, and production for export of luxury fruits and vegetables was introduced as an ill-fated and short-lived effort to redress the foreign agricultural trade imbalance (Barkin 1982; Barkin and Suárez 1985; Austin and Esteva 1987). This transformation converted Mexico into an important buyer of basic grains and powdered milk on world markets and resulted in substantial reductions in nutritional levels for important segments of the population.

In industry, too, the changes have been spectacular: Since 1962, the government focused its industrialization strategy around a domestic automobile production program (Lifschitz 1984; Jenkins 1986). The country enjoyed a dynamic rhythm of industrial growth: an average of 7.6 percent per year during the two decades before the onset of the first modern crisis in 1976. But the distribution of industrial growth among sectors (Table 5.3) was clearly oriented toward a small segment of the population—perhaps 30 percent or less in the middle and upper classes, who bathed in the reflected light of extraordinarily concentrated prosperity for several decades.[3] In contrast, the slow growth of traditional food

TABLE 5.3

Structure of Industrial Production and Growth, 1960–1988 (percentages)

	Productive Structure[a]			Annual Growth	
	1960	1980	1988	1960-80	1980-88
All manufacturing[b]	48.3	988.9	1,056	7.62	0.82
Industrial Sectors					
1. Food & beverage	33.9	24.6	26.2	5.69	1.62
2. Textiles & clothing	16.1	13.8	11.6	6.22	−1.32
3. Wood & wood products	4.2	4.3	3.8	6.40	−0.64
4. Paper & printing	5.0	5.5	5.9	7.76	1.78
5. Chemicals, petroleum products, and rubber	15.3	14.9	18.1	9.49	3.31
6. Nonmetalic mineral products	5.1	7.0	7.0	8.23	0.86
7. Basic metal industries	5.6	6.2	6.3	7.68	1.12
8. Metal products, machinery, and equipment	13.2	21.3	18.7	10.21	−0.81
Selected Industries					
1. Animal feed	1.2	1.2	0.5	8.04	−10.70
Beer and liquor	4.8	4.1	3.7	6.79	−0.54
Soft drinks	1.6	1.7	2.3	8.17	4.48
2. Thread and yarn	5.3	3.9	4.2	5.94	0.93
Clothing	3.9	4.1	3.7	7.94	−0.50
5. Petroleum, petrochemicals	4.1	5.1	3.3	8.87	−4.62
Basic chemicals	0.7	1.3	1.6	10.48	3.42
Fertilizers	0.3	0.6	0.4	11.93	−2.55
Synthetic resins	0.7	3.0	2.3	15.54	−2.18
Pharmaceuticals	2.9	3.3	2.0	8.31	2.21
Soaps and cosmetics	1.7	2.0	2.2	8.44	2.45
Rubber products	2.2	2.6	1.8	8.49	−3.20
6. Glass and cement	1.8	2.5	2.9	9.41	2.92
8. Nonelectrical machinery	2.0	3.4	2.9	10.67	−1.47
Electrical machinery	1.0	1.3	1.3	9.30	0.24
Home appliances	0.5	1.6	0.6	14.16	−10.40
Electronics	1.4	2.7	1.7	11.36	−4.91
Electrical equipment	0.8	1.1	1.0	9.16	−0.67
Automobiles	1.7	3.8	3.8	12.15	0.83
Car parts	0.5	2.7	3.0	17.22	2.43

[a]Share of manufacturing output generated by sector or subsector.
[b]Hundreds of millions of 1980 pesos.

Source: SPP (Secretaría de Programación y Presupuesto), INEGI (Instituto Nacional de Estadística, Geográfia, e Informática), *Sistema de Cuentas Nacionales de México, 1960–1985, 1985–1988*, Mexico City: SPP, INEGI, 1986, 1990.

and beverage industries (sector 1 in Table 5.3), with the exception of animal feed and alcoholic beverages, is a reflection of the stagnant demand for basic food products by most Mexicans despite the widespread problems of malnutrition throughout the society.

The high growth rates of sectors 5, 6, and 8 stem from effective government policies that emphasized developing basic industries and consumer durables oriented to the demands of a small elite of large industrial capitalists and wealthy consumer groups. Among the industries that benefited from this rapid growth were, naturally, automobile and auto parts manufacturers along with producers of electro-domestic appliances and electronic equipment. Similarly, the accelerated growth of the modern components of chemical and petroleum derivative sectors (petrochemicals, basic chemicals, fertilizers, and synthetic resins) points to the growing influence of modern basic industries that produce goods for an elite of heavily capitalized industries like plastics and synthetic fabrics as well as for farmers and ranchers.

Continuing Import Dependence

The Mexican pattern of industrialization occasioned a heavy drain on potential capital formation because of dependence on imports. Since Mexico's industrial structure is still not well integrated, the expansion of industrial production required increasing imports of basic machinery and even intermediate raw materials and components for the domestic assembly of manufactured goods. Raw material imports rose from 32 percent of the total imports in 1954 to almost 60 percent in 1980. The automobile assembly and parts industry alone accounted for as much as $3 billion of the foreign trade deficit of $4.9 billion in 1979. The steel industry, in spite of a heavy government investment program, had also become an increasing drain on the balance of payments, requiring net imports of basic inputs equivalent to as much as 10 percent of the value of its total domestic steel production (Restrepo 1984). Evidence of the increasing import dependence of this pattern of import-substituting industrialization is widely available (e.g., Valenzuela Feijóo 1986). Moreover, industrial exports had not become substantially diversified by the early 1980s despite substantial subsidies and promotion efforts to generate export earnings to offset the cost of imported inputs. Before the boom in petroleum exports, unprocessed minerals accounted for a growing proportion of total exports; the growth of oil exports expanded this category (which includes petroleum) to more than three-quarters of Mexico's total exports. Even the highly touted and government subsidized *maquiladora*, or border assembly industry, employed about 1.5 percent of the labor force at the beginning of the 1980s; this industry may not have made a net contribution to the country's balance of payments before the substantial 1982 devaluation because most *maquila* workers bought their daily necessities primarily in the United States.

Tax Policy as a Reflection of Political Weakness

Finally, government taxation policies further polarized Mexican society. Because of the government's inability to broaden its revenue base by taxing the income of the rich and the profits of the growing industrial sector, the treasury has depended for its income on taxing a very narrow base: middle-class consumption, foreign trade, and salaried wage earners. Until the mid-1980s, the government has systematically been unable to impose substantial taxes on profits because of powerful opposition from the capitalists; the policy makers justified their position by claiming that profit taxes would discourage private productive investment. As a result, the government resorted to raising revenues by increasing taxes on salaried incomes and consumption; contributions from income taxes— paid primarily by salaried workers—rose from less than 10 percent to more than 36 percent of government revenues between 1940 and 1980, while sales taxes, now replaced by a value-added tax, burgeoned from practically nothing to 17 percent of the total. These modifications have exacerbated the regressiveness of the Mexican tax structure because only wage earners with an income above the official minimum wage and captive consumers of national products are systematically taxed, without any form of relief from relatively high tax rates.[4] In spite of repeated tax reform efforts and improved collection procedures, these revenue sources proved inadequate to finance official expenditures, obliging the government to search constantly for additional sources of revenue for its programs.

For the government, foreign funding proved an excellent, low-cost expedient. But such funding was highly inflationary and revealed political frailty. The deadlock in negotiations between government, workers, and capitalists made it impossible to either increase taxes on the rich or even persuade them to finance the deficit internally by buying government bonds. Foreign support for local deficit financing permitted the Mexican state to postpone the day of reckoning. Instead of attempting to correct the sectoral imbalances in production or to confront directly the growing unrest and social disparities—which became patently obvious in the violent confrontations between the state and many social groups in 1968—foreign-financed military pressure, public expenditures, and demagoguery became the tools of choice. The government's inability to resolve the underlying social conflicts led to rising government budget deficits that were financed by borrowing from private foreign banks, which were

TABLE 5.4
Structure of Public Sector Investment, 1940–1988 (percentages)

	1940	1950	1960	1970	1980	1988[a]
Agriculture	15	19	8	13	17	9
Industry	21	30	37	38	46	42
Transport and communications	52	40	30	20	12	22
Social welfare	10	10	23	27	22	22
Defense and administration	2	1	2	2	3	5
Public investment as share of GDP	3.7	5.2	5.6	7.0	10.1	4.6
Public investment as share of total capital formation	49.1	50.0	32.8	32.9	43.0	27.3

[a]The sectoral structure refers to 1986.

Sources: NAFINSA (Nacional Financiera, S.A.), *La Economía Mexicana en Cifras*, Mexico City: NAFINSA, 1978; SPP (Secretaría de Programación y Presupuesto), INEGI (Instituto Nacional de Estadística, Geográfia, e Informática), *El Ingreso y Gasto Público en México*, Mexico City: SPP, INEGI, 1986; SPP, INEGI, *Sistema de Cuentas Nacionales de México, 1960–1985, 1985–1988*, Mexico City: SPP, INEGI, 1986, 1990.

anxious to lend the growing volumes of petro-dollars being channeled into their vaults from the OPEC countries. This process rapidly accelerated inflationary pressures in the mid-1970s.[5] The announcement of the oil discoveries in 1976 arrived like a *deus ex machina*, permitting the new president, José López Portillo, to further postpone resolution of the underlying inherited social and economic imbalances by "administering the new prosperity." The situation reached crisis proportions in 1982 when oil prices dropped again and private foreign financial support was withdrawn.

Public investment accentuated the problem of social polarization (Table 5.4). Rather than redressing the growing inequalities in the society, public investment programs directly promoted the productive investments controlled by the wealthiest segments of the national and international capitalist class. The increasing tightness of government funds since 1970 clearly showed official priorities: In the midst of sharp cutbacks in investment, the government offered expanding support for productive investments in manufacturing, especially in basic and export-oriented industries like automobiles, petroleum, cement, steel, and *maquila* operations, at the expense of investment in social welfare. Since the early 1980s, investments in the communications and transport sector—including the new satellite system and improved international telecommunications— have also taken priority over social welfare investments. Public expenditures for agriculture were mostly for large irrigation programs that benefited a well-heeled modern agricultural class that was producing for export at the expense of the vast majority of small farmers who were producing for domestic consumption. The upsurge in spending in agriculture in 1980 was an aberration, the result of the short-lived Mexican Food System designed to bolster production of basic grains (see Chapter 2).

The Contradictions of Mexican Development

Historically, capitalism has not permitted a long-term improvement in workers' living standards *at the expense of capital*. By the early 1970s, national and international capital judged that the wage levels and living standards of Mexican workers had risen too fast in relation to profit rates. This market view of the inflated living standards of workers was manifested in the inability of Mexican manufactured goods to compete on international markets with those produced in other countries where labor costs were lower. In response, financial groups decided to attempt to reverse the tendency by lowering real wages to reshape the Mexican economy to the needs of the consolidating global market. In this initial period, industrialists gave little consideration to the possibility of and need for increasing labor productivity through investments to modernize their plants and equipment, as an alternative to intensifying the level of conflict between labor and capital by demanding the implementation of a repressive wage policy, which began in 1977.

With the onset of national and international crises in 1976, the Mexican government had to rethink the country's role in the international economy. Development policy could not simply focus on assuring an adequate volume of investment funds; the discipline of the marketplace would no longer tolerate the simplistic response of past years—increasing government investment—when private investors were unwilling to broaden the nation's productive capacity. Instead, in the new global market in which Mexico was playing a growing role, the state's function was to reshape social relations to create an attractive environment that would stimulate industrialists—domestic and foreign—to invest in new competitive ventures, which would in turn allow the country to become a responsible participant in the international economy. This internationalization of capital has succeeded in lowering real wages and reorienting production to export commodities, benefiting the international financial community and allied Mexican business groups. By restraining wage increases below the rate of inflation and reorienting the government's role in the economy to investment promotion and crisis management while compressing government's historical role as the welfare state, these business groups also contributed to reshaping political forces within Mexico and redistributing income and power for their own benefit as they actively participated in the international economy. The contradictions created by the inwardly oriented development of past decades are now taking root and imposing a heavy tax on the country, a cost that is being paid by the Mexican working classes.

The myriad contradictions occasioned by decades of development with improving living standards provoked social and economic disequilibria throughout the society. Rising incomes and controlled prices for basic consumer goods made agricultural production unprofitable. In some regions government enterprises stepped in or were created to guarantee supplies, while in other zones food imports were required to meet demand. The private sector reoriented its production to respond to the newly created demands of the dynamic and large middle sectors. But even these vibrant internal markets offered low profit rates, leaving industrialists discouraged and inducing them to reduce investment and move their funds abroad.

The government was caught in an unresolvable conflict. Better education, the fuller incorporation of isolated regions into national life, and the rhetorical promises of popular participation in a democratic political process had raised expectations and aspirations. To fulfill the heightened hopes of Mexicans, the government needed to increase expenditures for social services and expand subsidies to maintain price stability in the face of rising costs and high profits. But public sector revenues were severely limited as investors, the only sector virtually outside the taxing system, continued to block any meaningful tax reform.

Externally, too, Mexican development encountered problems that were exacerbated by its own internal contradictions. Agricultural exports began to face some restrictive barriers in foreign markets, while domestic demand from the middle sectors absorbed an increasing share of production of new commercial products. Demands for beef, pork, and chicken by Mexico's wealthy and in foreign markets created a need for animal feeds, which used crops that displaced basic food crops for human consumption in some of the most fertile, productive regions of the country. In the search for new ways to increase output, ranchers discovered the Mexican tropics and introduced inefficient forms of extensive cattle grazing there, at the expense of denuding millions of hectares of irretrievable tropical rainforest. In the 1970s, the domestic manufacturing sector proved itself uninterested and too inefficient to compete in international markets; instead, it became an ever more burdensome drain on the country's foreign account as the sector imported ever-greater quantities of costly raw materials, intermediate products, and capital equipment. At the same time, growing volumes of basic agricultural imports in the 1970s converted the agricultural sector into another drain on foreign exchange, reversing its long history of contributing to foreign exchange earnings. The changing productive structure resulted in a dramatic increase in imports of basic consumer goods during the 1970s, from 7 percent of the total import bill in 1970 to 13 percent in 1980 and 15 percent in 1989.

Thus, the need to search for foreign capital grew progressively, as domestic resources were insufficient to offset government expenditures and foreign trade occasioned a growing imbalance. External savings in the form of foreign investments or loans were needed to make up the difference. The significant feature of the early 1970s was that the international financial community was willing, even anxious, and able to provide the needed financing because of the sudden influx of money from the OPEC nations that set the international banking system scrambling to create profitable investments. Already an attractive borrower and a favorite of the official multilateral financial agencies because of its political stability and its favorable performance as a model of capitalist development, in the mid-1970s Mexico became a magnet for international lending as a result of the announcement of vast petroleum reserves.

Fat with oil money and foreign lending, Mexico could increase spending to defuse domestic conflicts over government largess and attempts to defend real incomes, which in another era would have had to have been resolved through internal political struggles over the distribution of available resources. New expenditure or subsidy programs, the easing of restrictive import barriers, and liberalized economic policies for new investment were instruments adopted to further postpone the day of reckoning. All of these alternatives either cost money or increased overall inefficiency of the bureaucracy and the industrial plant, but external resources were available in seemingly unlimited amounts to finance the expansive new policies. The developed countries' paranoia about possible further cartel action to continue to raise the price of petroleum fueled Mexico's optimism and its carefree attitude toward spending. The government aimed to satisfy the demands of many groups of working people and others while it also embarked on a very costly program of industrial restructuring based on rapid expansion of the petroleum sector.

International capital joined with domestic entrepreneurs beginning in the late 1970s to found new industries oriented toward manufacturing for export markets. Similarly, capitalist farmers were encouraged to look abroad for sales. New private sector industrial projects sprung up along with ambitious petrochemical and steel development programs by government enterprises to spark a new wave of construction. But the industrial construction boom only worsened already severe bottlenecks in industries supplying materials and in labor markets created by the upsurge in construction of basic infrastructure needed to export the petroleum that was expected to eventually finance the expanding public sector. To some observers the changing productive structure was a source of concern, while to others it was a mark of progress and modernity.

The tensions and inconsistencies brought on by the oil and borrowing boom were there for all to see. The growing foreign debt was public knowledge. Public sector deficits were suddenly a subject of open debate and engendered vociferous reprimands from impotent legislators. Frustrated smallholders vainly sought federal resources to make their lands productive again, and workers ineffectually struggled to maintain the real value of their wages in the face of accelerating inflation. Investors, and even some of the middle sectors, responded to the government's evident inability to control the situation by taking billions of dollars out of the country, thereby converting the government and the banking system into a conduit to attract international capital to the country, which was then drained into private fortunes in foreign accounts.

During the first years of the 1980s, the intensifying national debate about the appropriate road to follow forewarned of the dangers of the policies adopted. In the face of intense criticism and profound conflict, the government's expansionary policies lasted as long as they did only because of the international banking community's own greed. The foreign bankers' desire to lend unprecedented volumes of speculative capital led them to add their own lack of discipline to that of the power brokers on the Mexican scene. In August 1982, Mexico closed its foreign exchanges and declared a temporary moratorium on its debt service because of events beyond its borders: falling oil prices, rising international interest rates, and even recessionary tendencies in the richer countries. The subsequent nationalization of the banking system and the implementation of a series of unprecedented austerity programs set the stage for a further round of productive restructuring and social repression in Mexico as called for by international capital during the previous decade. This restructuring continues to be the principal chore for the Mexican state on the eve of the 1990s. After almost a decade of such policies, however, the question still at hand is whether a better alternative exists for the Mexican people. After I describe the wake of social destruction left by the onslaught of austerity in the 1980s in the next chapter, I conclude this book with a concrete program for restoring Mexico to prosperity while keeping it a responsible member of the international community.

Notes

1. I include the 1984 income distribution data for comparison, but since the data include substantial amounts of imputed in-kind incomes, such as the rental value of owner-occupied housing and on-farm consumption, the series makes it appear that there was a substantial decline in inequality. In fact, the opposite is true: Incomes were more unequally distributed in the 1980s than previously.

2. When the banking system was nationalized, the sizable nonfinancial assets of the banks were "unbundled" and eventually sold back to the private sector.

3. It is important to note that 30 percent of the Mexican population—20 to 28 million people during the 1960–1990 period of industrialization—is larger than the total population of many advanced countries and thus offers an important market for industrial production, even though it is a small part of the total Mexican population.

4. The personal income-tax structure is highly progressive and allows virtually no deductions except for medical expenses; in 1989, a full-time senior university professor would pay a marginal rate of about 40 percent, down from 48 percent a decade earlier, as a result of a decline in purchasing power of more than 50 percent. But income from capital, including capital gains on the booming stock exchange, went untaxed.

5. For a further explanation of this analysis of inflation see Barkin and Esteva (1979, 1986).

6

Stabilization Policy: The Destabilization of Mexico

In this chapter I explore the underlying tenets of the economic programs adopted during the 1982–1989 period in Mexico and evaluate the several stabilization programs in terms of their impact on the country's long-range capacity to resolve the fundamental structural imbalances that are the root causes of the present crisis.

The Origins of the Crisis

The seeds of Mexico's continuing economic crisis were sown in the early postwar period (1945–1960) when Mexico embarked on a long-term development strategy to industrialize its predominantly agricultural economy. This strategy was based on several fundamental, but erroneous, assumptions about the nature of the development process. First, the import substitution–industrialization scheme presupposed the desirability of forging a new productive structure to supply the commodities consumed by a small group of wealthy people at the time these policies were being formulated. Second, the policy makers assumed that, once given control of some land, the peasants would become acquiescent producers of the nation's food supply rather than be profoundly transformed by the market economy into rational, small-scale producers who would reduce their production should it become unprofitable. Third, the government accepted investor demands for protection and subsidies, thereby guaranteeing high rates of profitability for new industrial ventures. The corollary to the deal cut with private entrepreneurs was that the government assumed responsibility for producing many basic goods and services that required large or risky investments. Finally, international capital and transnational firms were accepted as essential ingredients in the development of many consumer and intermediate goods industries.

Each of these assumptions proved to be incorrect. The strategy shaped an industrial structure that produced primarily consumer goods for the middle class and the wealthy, including food products, household appliances, cosmetics, and, eventually, automobiles. This stimulated production that was ill suited to the needs of most Mexicans, who remained poor. When the policy makers chose automobile assembly to be the backbone of the country's industrial production strategy in the early 1960s, the industry and associated producers in such sectors as steel, glass, and rubber were unable to create as many jobs as expected. Furthermore, the automotive complex did not become the engine of the new industrialization program because most Mexicans could not acquire the new domestically assembled vehicles and they were too expensive to compete on international markets. Though demands from middle-class consumers burgeoned, the industrialization program failed to stimulate the production of socially necessary goods and services, such as inexpensive and high-quality mass consumer goods, public transport systems, and urban infrastructures.

Industrial development programs provided credits and other incentives to stimulate the installation of new industries during the 1960s. In this profitable environment, private investment joined with foreign interests to install new factories based on foreign, relatively capital-intensive production systems, producing goods for an affluent minority. In spite of a nationalistic discourse, much of the country's new productive structure has been shaped, if not owned, by transnational firms; equipment embodying new technologies and labor processes has contributed to higher productivity and profits, but also has led to greater difficulty in employing large numbers of new entrants into the Mexican labor force. The developmental costs and financial stimuli were paid for by poor and middle-income taxpayers or by foreign borrowing, as the government was unable to tax the wealthy.

As postrevolutionary land distribution programs slowed in the 1970s, small-farmer production of basic food crops declined. Government programs and financial resources stimulated fruit and vegetable output for the wealthy consumers in Mexico and for export. As a consequence, Mexico has spent billions of dollars to import millions of tons of foodstuffs that could have been produced domestically, which would have freed foreign exchange to be used to service the debt and to promote a more balanced internal development scheme.

The Stabilization Program

Stabilization efforts focused on the need to control inflation. The government's main instruments in this task were its ability to restrain wage demands and government spending while managing the value of the peso and domestic interest rates, rather than letting the market reign in the financial arena. The growth of the monetary supply was also held in check by draconian measures to reduce government spending and by channeling domestic savings to finance the government budget. By putting a tight lid on the annual tripartite (government, labor, and management) negotiations that focused on the minimum wage, policy makers were able to exert a decisive influence in controlling wage increases throughout the economy. Similarly, policy makers implemented draconian reductions in social programs and curbs on employment, along with important increases in the prices for government goods and services (the most important being prices for energy and transport, but also extending to basic food products). After acceding to a sharp devaluation of the peso in 1982, financial authorities attempted to manage the decline in the peso during the following years by fixing internal interest rates and stimulating exports while sharply restricting imports. Government economists implicitly assumed that this would demonstrate the government's capacity to manage the economy and, consequently, strengthen investor confidence.

The policy to restrict wage increases affected the lower and middle-income groups most heavily. Official determinations of the evolution of the minimum wage serve as a benchmark for labor contract settlements throughout the economy. Since 1982, the governmental Minimum Wage Commission that sets the rate has institutionalized a steady and substantial decline in the purchasing power of wages (Figure 6.1). In the most recent period (1983–1986), however, these figures understate the real deterioration in many incomes, because most organized workers who earned more than the minimum wage received an even smaller percentage increase than the minimum wage hike and their living costs rose more than the official consumer's price index indicated. A review of the history of minimum wages (Figure 6.1) shows that they have fallen dramatically, by more than 50 percent during the 1983–1989 period, leaving the real purchasing power of the minimum wage in 1989 at about two-thirds of the level prevailing in 1970. (For the privileged minority of salaried workers who earn more than the minimum, purchasing power has declined even more because their wages have declined relative to the minimum wage.)

The real earning power of the majority of small farmers suffered similar or even greater declines. Mexico's growing inability to supply itself with its own basic foodstuffs despite an abundance of idle land and underemployed rural workers is testimony to the lack of profitability of even the most rudimentary work for millions of peasants. In contrast, when the profitability of producing basic grains increased in 1981–1982, maize output increased 19 percent along with other crops sown by small

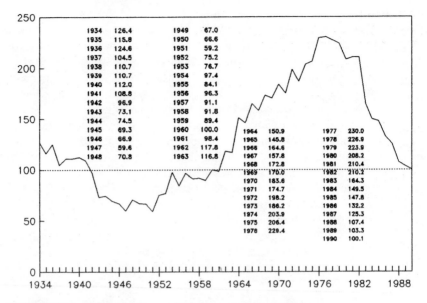

FIGURE 6.1 Real Minimum Salaries, 1934–1990

Note: 1960 = 100.

Source: National Minimum Salary Commission, internal working documents.

farmers. In the 1980s, as prices have risen, these farmers continue to raise maize but they do so primarily for their own use rather than for sale at low prices in tightly controlled national markets.

Finally, the short-term adjustment policies adopted since 1982 have led to substantial increases in open and disguised unemployment. Quantitative measures of the growth of unemployment are open to question, but one respected student of the Mexican economy has estimated that urban open unemployment increased from 5.8 percent at the beginning of 1982 to an average of over 10 percent at the end of 1984 (Bortz 1985). At the same time, other indicators of underemployment—such as the massive abandonment or declining intensity of cultivation of rainfed lands, steep declines in construction industries, and a sizable increase in the number of people who had been gainfully employed but are now no longer even looking for work (discouraged workers)—suggest that the hardship imposed by a decline in earnings is compounded by the difficulty of finding employment in the formal sector. In contrast, local studies throughout the country demonstrate that families are compensating for declining opportunities by expanding their informal activities

TABLE 6.1
Growth Rates of Manufacturing Industries, 1980–1988

	Annual Rates of Growth		
	1980-1982	1982-1985	1985-1988
All manufacturing	1.9	0.9	0.1
Flour	5.2	2.9	0.1
Meat	4.3	0.7	−1.5
Beer	1.9	−0.3	4.8
Clothing	−1.1	−0.9	−3.1
Home appliances	1.6	−10.9	−2.7
Automobiles	−5.2	−1.5	4.3
Car parts	0.5	4.9	−0.7
Capital goods	−3.0	−2.8	0.9
Glass, cement	−0.3	2.8	3.1
Steel	−2.4	1.2	1.4

Source: SPP (Secretaría de Programación y Presupuesto), INEGI (Instituto Nacional de Estadística, Geográfia, e Informática), *Sistema de Cuentas Nacionales de México, 1960–1985, 1985–1988*, Mexico City: SPP, INEGI, 1986, 1990.

in artisan and home production, contract work, and commerce, as well as by increasing the frequency with which family members search for employment in the United States, either as part of the new U.S. amnesty program or as undocumented workers. As a result, a larger number of people in many households are finding ways to contribute to family income or production in order to slow the decline in their real living standards. (In these circumstances, and with available data, it is virtually impossible to determine whether labor force participation rates are increasing.)

The unequal impact of these effects of stabilization policy on the nation's welfare and the distribution of the fruits of production can be measured with several indirect indicators. Among the poorest people, per capita consumption of milk and other dairy products, meats, eggs, and even beans has fallen sharply in the 1980s, as real incomes declined. Among the middle strata (bureaucrats, lawyers, doctors, other professionals, and the organized labor force), purchases of consumer durables declined precipitously, while production of luxury automobiles for the rich and of auto parts rose (Table 6.1) because those business groups that survived enjoyed continued prosperity. Capital flight increased dramatically from an average of about $1.5 billion during the 1973–1979 period to more than $10.2 billion in the 1980–1984 period (see Table 6.3). My estimates of capital flight are even greater, including additional unreported sources of foreign exchange earnings and withdrawals resulting from transfer pricing, underinvoicing of exports, and overinvoicing of imports (Chapter 4). In conclusion, then, we can see that the stabilization policies themselves have extracted a substantial sacrifice from the majority of poor and middle-income groups while privileging a very small group of industrialists, commercial farmers, and professionals and draining the country of vital investment capital.

The Nature of Stabilization Policies

During the López Portillo administration (1976–1982), the Mexican government hoped to resolve some of the profound inherited social and economic problems with revenues from international oil sales. It set out to use the newly acknowledged wealth to accelerate the development of its industrial potential. But it is now clear that the government overinvested in infrastructure for the oil industry and selected a poor mix of industries (petrochemicals, cement, steel) on which to construct a basis for future growth. Of course, it also misjudged the impact of international competition on prices. The heritage of debt, inflation, and greater social inequality that resulted from misguided petroleum industry plans will continue to weigh heavily on the country for decades.

During the Miguel de la Madrid presidency (1982–1988), Mexico's economic program responded to the demands of the International Monetary Fund and the world banking community. In fact, in 1983 and 1984, Mexico was hailed by the international financial institutions as the prime example of responsible economic restructuring and as a model debtor. Mexico refused to participate in the (abortive) regional efforts to create a debtors club at the 1986 Cartagena meeting, and in 1985 Mexico rushed funds to Argentina to head off a debt moratorium when the U.S. Federal Reserve System delayed granting a temporary loan during particularly difficult negotiations. For these efforts Mexico was rewarded with an attractive package for restructuring its foreign debt that extended payments over a longer period and lowered interest payments. Foreign banks also accepted a substantial reduction in their normal commissions for such an operation, which amounted to a reported savings of several hundred million dollars.

Since that time, debt renegotiation has continued to be one of the main factors shaping economic policy formulation in Mexico. Along with efforts to stretch out the repayment period, Mexico joined the ranks of countries allowing foreign investors to purchase their debt at a steep discount (45 percent) on world financial markets, which was seen as a way of allowing foreign investors to finance their investments in Mexico. This controversial program lasted only two years because of the profound inflationary impact brought on by the injection of as much as $2 billion of new currency into the economy without any short-term increase in domestic output.

The presidential transition in late 1988 did not bring any substantial modification in economic policy formulation. This prompted many political analysts to suggest that it was Carlos Salinas de Gortari who actually controlled the reins during the second half of the previous administration. The widely heralded debt negotiations during 1989 under the shadow of the Brady Plan provided substantially less relief than was needed. Mexico continued to be hailed as an exemplary member of the international community, but the promised inflow of new funds could not be used to stimulate economic growth for fear that the specter of inflation would unravel the tenuous *pactos* imposed on unwilling participants by an imperious government.

The domestic economic policies that evoked this favorable international response produced a redistribution of income and economic activity that favored Mexico's elites to the detriment of the rest of the population. By slashing the public sector deficit (from 17.6 percent of national product in 1982 to 8.9 percent in 1983 and 5.7 percent in 1984), reducing real wages substantially, and curtailing bank credit, the government succeeded in bringing inflation down from almost 100 percent in 1982 to 81 percent in 1983 and 59 percent in 1984. The poor suffered most in the budget-cutting process, which curtailed many social services and eliminated subsidies for many basic foodstuffs. When the federal deficit rose to 9.5 percent in 1985, inflation climbed only 5 percent, to 64 percent, but it took off again in 1986 and 1987, reaching over 150 percent as government spending continued to outpace revenues. As inflation eroded the internal market and production costs fell due to successive large devaluations of the peso, the current-account of the balance of payments was reversed from a substantial deficit of almost $6 billion in 1982 to a surplus of $5.3 billion, $4.0 billion, and $500 million in the following three years. Economic growth, which had been −0.5 percent in 1982 and −5.3 percent in 1983, rose to 3.7 percent in 1984 and 2.7 percent in 1985, occasioning fears that the country's public managers had, in fact, once again lost control of the situation, this time by allowing the economy to overheat. But the precipitous fall of oil prices in 1986 undercut previous gains and pushed the economy down into negative growth once again.

This history reflects the policy makers' conviction that their efforts to make major adjustments in the domestic economy had been successful and that the solution to the country's problems now lay in the hands of the international market. Their strategy and hopes centered around securing more credit at easier terms, attracting foreign investment, and improving Mexico's access to international markets. The obvious prescription for achieving these results was the neoliberal approach to policy formulation: opening the domestic economy, joining the GATT, diversifying exports to reduce dependence on oil, and reducing oil prices below prevailing levels posted officially by OPEC.

Little attention was directed toward domestic production. Bank credit for expanding industrial and agricultural output was severely restricted, especially in the rural areas, where only the most affluent of the commercial farmers were able to obtain needed financial resources. Heavy restrictions were placed on credit for industrial production; combined with the contraction of the domestic market, manufacturing output experienced a sharp fall during 1982–1983. A slight recuperation followed in 1984–1985, led by special incentives directed at stimulating automobile and auto parts production as a unique beneficiary. The results are evident in the aggregate statistics and in the differential growth results for each industry during the 1980s (Table 6.2). Similarly, the data on investment in machinery and equipment show that automobile purchases increased 35.4 percent in 1985 while output of domestic manufactured machinery grew only 3.6 percent in 1984, although it climbed to 15.4 percent in 1985. Imported capital equipment increased 25 percent as a result of the progressive liberalization of international trade (Bank of México, *Informe Anual 1985*, Mexico City: Banco de México, 1986).

The effort to rebuild the economy in the 1980s was concentrated on the automobile industry and on widening the export base, primarily with new investments from abroad. The labor-intensive manufacturing assembly plants (*maquiladores*) were also supported and some new operations were built away from the northern border, where environmental problems and labor shortages sometimes offset the cost advantages of geographic proximity. Government investment was severely restricted except to stimulate these priority areas for private investment.

The austerity program clearly did not affect all sectors equally. Workers and small farmers suffered a dramatic and rapid decline in their living standards as wages and basic grain prices lagged behind skyrocketing inflation. Government spending could not be held in check as originally planned because certain privileged sectors—especially well-organized consumer and worker groups in Mexico City—were consistently able to prevent cutbacks from impacting them as greatly as planned. Thus, the stimulus from the public sector continued to be greater than planned, and in 1985 the deficit (as a proportion of GDP) was once again climbing toward the 9.5 percent level and exerting a consequent upward pressure

TABLE 6.2
Aggregate Indicators of Mexican Economy, 1980–1988,
GDP by Sectors (structure and annual growth rates)

	1980	1982	1985	1988	Annual Rates of Growth		
					1980-1982	1982-1985	1985-1988
Agriculture	9.0	8.8	8.5	8.0	3.0	4.3	-1.8
Oil industry	1.3	1.3	0.6	0.7	6.0	6.7	5.2
Non-oil industry	33.9	34.0	31.1	30.8	4.1	-0.8	-0.4
Commerce & service	57.1	57.1	61.1	61.5	3.9	0.1	0.0
TOTAL GDP	100	100	100	100	4.3	0.5	-0.3

Source: SPP (Secretaría de Programación y Presupuesto), INEGI (Instituto Nacional de Estadística, Geográfia, e Informática), *Sistema de Cuentas Nacionales de México, 1960–1985, 1985–1988,* Mexico City: SPP, INEGI, 1986, 1990.

on price levels. The foreign account actually produced a greater surplus than originally planned in 1983 and 1984, as imports fell more drastically than expected with the erosion of the internal market and the absence of a private sector response to pleas for more investment and modernization.

Perhaps the most important failure of the early stabilization programs, in the final analysis, was their inability to instill a measure of confidence in the regime's capacity to manage the economy. Despite its responsiveness to the prescriptions of the international financial community, the Mexican stabilization program failed to inspire the confidence of Mexican entrepreneurs, who reduced their own investment sharply.

The lack of cooperation from the wealthiest groups of society set off a significant drain of resources. During the late 1970s and 1980s, the richest financial and industrial groups led a massive assault on Mexico's investment capital and foreign reserves, transferring tens of billions of dollars out of the country in a dramatic demonstration of lack of confidence in official policies and in the government's capacity to effectively manage the crisis. From 1983 onward, the *whole* of annual net private savings was being invested abroad; in fact, capital flight reached such proportions that some people actually liquidated their productive assets for expatriation (Table 6.3). The *Wall Street Journal* reported an international banker's estimate "that Mexican businesses squirreled away as much as $5 billion during the first six-months of last year [1984] alone by this method" (October 11, 1985) of faking foreign trade invoices. If the more than $50 billion in flight capital (plus the accrued earnings from profits and interest) had been available for domestic investment from 1976 to 1985, Mexico could have more than doubled its historically recorded rates of capital formation while also reducing net foreign indebtedness. In reality, capital formation fell while the country's foreign debt rose.

The Design of the New Economy

The stabilization programs of the 1980s have accelerated the Mexican process of internationalization (Rozo and Barkin 1983; Barkin 1985). The country has moved beyond the narrow confines of past development strategies that promoted import-substituting industrialization and job creation via the *maquila* program; the new programs are accelerating Mexico's integration into the international economy. This involves a reshaping of production processes, including the assimilation of new technologies and a new organization of the labor process, which involves more automation and fewer workers in production. Consumption patterns are being altered to include more animal proteins and processed foods, both of which are increasingly out of the reach of the majority.

TABLE 6.3
Private Capital Flight and
Mexican-owned Foreign Assets, 1973–1984

	Private Capital Flight	Stock of Foreign Assets Held by Mexicans
1973	1.0	3.0
1974	1.3	4.0
1975	1.3	5.2
1976	3.4	8.6
1977	1.3	9.8
1978	1.3	11.2
1979	2.1	13.2
1980	4.8	18.0
1981	15.0	38.0
1982	14.4	47.4
1983	8.5	55.9
1984	8.1	64.0

Sources: Jaime Ros, "Mexico: From the Oil Boom to the Debt Crisis," in Laurence Whitehead and Rosemary Thorp, eds., *The Debt Crisis in Latin America*, London: Macmillan, 1986, Table 15; corrections using estimates of unrepatriated returns of Mexican-owned foreign assets.

Official attempts to diminish the strains of past growth (1955–1980) have further heightened the contradictions. As a strategy for overcoming the crisis, the present regime chose to continue to emphasize international economic integration and to respond to the consumption demands of the rich. The majority of Mexicans have less income and must work longer hours than at the beginning of the 1980s. The economy is less capable of producing the basic goods and services required, even at its presently depressed levels. Stabilization has not achieved even its short-term objectives, and it has also moved the society further away from dealing with the fundamental necessity of feeding the population and attending to its other basic requirements, such as generating employment, maintaining health and nutritional standards, and protecting the environment. The polarization of Mexican society, reflected in the indicators reviewed in this chapter, only portends a further heightening of social struggle, which up to now has been held in check by the creative mobilization of the entire panoply of policy tools available to the government. In this sense, stabilization is destabilizing because it sets in motion a process of depletion of government resources and response mechanisms.

I have argued that the present strategy of development is unsustainable because it reduces basic production for the Mexicans without providing alternative sources of employment or new ways for people to survive (Barkin and Suárez 1985). It creates growing disequilibria, and these disequilibria must be corrected before Mexico can emerge from the crisis. The country is not capable of simply opening itself to a world economy in which Mexican workers must compete directly with the lowest paid workers in the third world. Mexican workers have a long history of achieving real gains in their living standards through prolonged mobilization (Barkin and Esteva 1979); regardless of the success of the attempts to roll back some of these achievements, it seems difficult to believe that other governments in the third world cannot be more successful in extracting greater productivity at a lower cost than is possible in the Mexican setting. The tradition of active political opposition to repression since the Mexican Revolution and in the course of years of highly organized labor activity is much more developed in Mexico than elsewhere.

A new orientation toward a viable economic development strategy must be based on mobilizing the country's own resources and its labor force. The only meaningful way to conceive of stabilization in the present world scene is to elaborate a development program that offers the possibility of further development. Given Mexico's relative affluence, its abundant natural resources, and its diversified economy, it need not reduce the output of current export and *maquila* industries in order to promote new ones. The result of accelerating Mexico's integration into the world economy is to erode the possibility of using the country's productive potential for resolving the most immediate and pressing productive and employment needs. New programs for modern economic development will not create sufficient permanent employment or generate sufficient demand to affect the depressed consumer sector.

An alternative approach based on revitalizing Mexico's rural economy could create millions of new productive jobs with sufficient levels of income to permit these producers to become consumers. The induced demand in light industry, construction, and services would create additional jobs while further strengthening an alternative development strategy based on the massive incorporation of the country's working population into productive occupations. The resources needed for such an approach are presently available. They could come from a redistribution of existing subsidies and from the use of resources now used for imports because domestic production is depressed. Such an approach would also give the small farmers much greater visibility and importance in the Mexican political scene. This alternative strategy is discussed in depth in the next chapter.

7

The War Economy Revisited: A Mexican Option in the 1990s

A new economic strategy—the war economy—could wrest Mexico from the throes of its present economic crisis. Without abandoning existing policies, the government could use the new approach to correct present social and economic imbalances by increasing food production to supply local markets and raising real wages to reverse the dramatic fall in purchasing power of recent years. The policy measures proposed in this chapter would spark a process of economic growth that not only would raise incomes of every social group but also would reduce the government budget deficit and improve the nation's foreign trade account. In this chapter, I provide some insights as to why such an approach has not been adopted up to now and discuss what steps would be necessary to implement the war economy strategy. Finally, I show how such a strategy would contribute to rekindling the nation's economic growth while productively incorporating millions of Mexicans into the labor force.

The Present Impasse

Since 1982, Mexico's economic crisis has idled nearly half of the industrial plants, thrown hundreds of thousands of Mexicans out of work, and reduced consumers' purchasing power by more than 35 percent. The economic restructuring has also brought about a reduction in the government work force, the selling off of many para-state firms, an easing of import restrictions, and an expansion of manufactured exports. The effects of what Mexicans universally call "the crisis" have created dislocations in every workplace, farming village, schoolroom, and household in the country.

The Mexican government continues to pursue its new export-led approach to recovery and growth of the economy. To compete in international markets, Mexico must produce different nontraditional goods

113

and lower their prices by reducing the cost of labor to foreigners. Ironically, during the 1980s these goals have been achieved with remarkable success: By sharply devaluing the peso and restraining wages, policy makers were increasing the volume of manufactured exports dramatically and temporarily reversing the nation's trade deficit. In spite of these important achievements, the light industry and farming sectors, which had been nurtured during two decades of "stabilizing development," are now floundering. Producers of light consumer goods for the burgeoning working and middle classes suddenly witnessed their markets vanish as real incomes fell particularly sharply among the nouveau riche of past epochs. Thousands of small farmers have been displaced or idled by discriminatory policies as better financed producers of animal feeds and cash crops for export took over resources formerly used to produce basic foods. The boom in outward-looking industrialization has been unable to compensate for layoffs and declining real incomes in the rest of the economy; as a result, Mexican society has become increasingly polarized, with islands of vitality in a morass of economic decline.

But policy makers seem unmoved by these contradictions. Recent stabilization or austerity programs continue to slash at real wages. These programs are incapable of stimulating economic growth with full employment because they are based on the incorrect assumption that the problems of the Mexican economy are financial and are predicated on concessions from the international banking community and government lenders. Rather than recognizing and attempting to reverse the country's fundamental problem—the progressive idling of its domestic productive capacity and its labor force—government authorities steadfastly insist on the need to respect international obligations (including the need to negotiate a reduction in the debt burden) which, in turn, requires further cuts in social programs, a cut in personnel, and continued declines in the population's purchasing power. The recurrent renegotiations of the value and maturity structure of the debt, the swap of foreign debt obligations for equity participation in domestic corporations, and other financial manipulations (such as the flawed exchange of present debt instruments for new ones backed by U.S. Treasury securities) have been important tools of crisis "management" since 1982. In spite of growing pressures from the U.S. government and the International Monetary Fund, private bankers are increasingly reluctant to provide fresh money to Mexico. In an atmosphere in which the lenders were becoming even more cautious and debtors were forced to be more aggressive in using their domestic problems as a bargaining chip, the World Bank Staff observes a growing "debt fatigue" that imperils negotiated settlements.[1]

The official analysis precludes a search for solutions among the masses of workers and small-scale rural producers. For the politicians, the crisis is a problem of too much debt, too little liquidity, and unfavorable international trade balances. In their view, political planning requires a careful balance between maintaining the country's good standing in international circles and searching for support among the competing political elites within the country. This approach is neither surprising nor unique to Mexico: It is the same one adopted throughout Latin America and supported from the world's major financial centers. Nowhere has it been particularly successful in resolving the underlying economic and social ills of the societies in which it has been applied.

The risks of not finding an alternative to existing approaches to rectify the imbalances in the economy are growing as austerity deepens. Mexico is Latin America's second largest debtor nation and makes the highest payments of debt service. The present monetarist adjustment process does not offer a long-term solution to the debt problem or to the broadening and deepening economic and social crisis. While some alternative arrangement must be negotiated for reducing debt service payments, Mexico must also make profound modifications in its present development strategy and productive structure, which brought on the debt and require repeated injections of new loans, ultimately increasing the debt burden.

A Mexican Option

The war economy strategy described in this chapter is intended as a contribution to the search for new approaches to reinitiate economic growth in Mexico. It is designed to improve rural welfare by stimulating food production and to replace imports that presently supply domestic consumers; the strategy also will increase the purchasing power of urban workers. This approach would complement and strengthen existing policies that promote the export of manufactured goods and the installation of labor-intensive manufacturing assembly plants (*maquila*); it would create a sustained growth of demand for light industrial goods, construction materials, and other products whose producers are among the leading victims of the stagnation provoked by current policy. The war economy can achieve these goals by stimulating increased output from idle lands and factories already in the hands of the producers. It is supposed that, with appropriate incentives (the promise of profits and higher wages), individuals will increase production in response to a national mobilization to overcome the crisis.

The Mexican war economy strategy would stimulate broad-based economic growth and put that growth on a sounder footing. The new impulse from growth would correct structural imbalances in the economy and free foreign exchange, which could be used to amortize the debt or increase growth further. The new strategy involves a profound reshaping of production for domestic consumption by recovering the country's existing underutilized productive potential. The strategy proposed in this chapter provides a means to correct the root causes of the country's present economic difficulties, strengthening rather than undermining Mexico's future economic development, by inviting the Mexican population to participate, with incentives, in expanding production and in helping alleviate the crisis for their families and for the nation as a whole.

The Origins and Prerequisites of the War Economy

The proposed strategy is similar to the war economy strategy that reorganized the British and U.S. economies during World War II. The political mobilization of productive potential in the hands of individuals was an orthodox (neoclassical) response to the inability of those economies to meet the needs of the civilian population during wartime. In Britain, the government organized a massive civilian mobilization of untapped productive capacity: Many workers contributed labor during their hours off, nonworking citizens joined the labor force, and families planted back yard "victory gardens" that ultimately replaced an important part of the fresh produce that Britain could no longer import because of the war at sea and the scarcity of ships for war materials.

The literature analyzing the British experience and the War Production Board in the United States makes it clear that in many situations government intervention is needed to create the conditions for the market to be able to function well. Under crisis conditions nonmarket mobilization of people and resources is needed. Two respected and orthodox study groups have pointed out that although the market works well under normal conditions, it "could scarcely be relied upon alone to accomplish the rapid and large structural changes which [were] needed" in wartime (Meade 1948:18; Director 1952). These changes were essential for achieving a fuller use of resources and ensuring that everyone enjoyed some of the benefits; but such changes must be implemented rapidly if they are not to be reversed by the inherent tendencies of the market to exacerbate rather than ameliorate any initial inequalities in the distribution of income, wealth, or power (Myrdal 1957:85).

Mexico is well endowed for implementing the structural changes required to boost food production and stimulate industrial output. The country possesses a large reservoir of underutilized resources that

Mexicans could easily bring into production. Available lands and factories could be used to promote renewed economic growth by producing a large volume of foodstuffs to replace current food imports and increasing the availability of manufactured consumer products. These measures would immediately improve the living standards of small-scale farmers in rainfed agricultural regions and of urban workers, who would be more fully occupied as a result of the program. By stimulating production of basic consumer goods to supply domestic needs, demand for other products (e.g., construction materials, agricultural machinery, industrial inputs, basic raw materials) would create spread effects that would rapidly integrate a widening circle of people and productive sectors into the growth process. Not only would such a strategy create more employment than any other single program, but its effects on the distribution of income would also be highly conducive to further sustainable growth.

Fortunately, there is striking evidence demonstrating the creativity and willingness of Mexicans, as individuals, to use their hidden reserves and hard work in order to survive throughout the crisis. Employed people have increased the number of hours they labor, and migration has increased sharply. As men left for the United States or for the Mexican cities in unprecedented numbers, women and children have been working in the fields or creating ways of earning money in the urban informal sector to eke out an existence as prices continue to rise faster than wages. And worker remittances from the United States and urban areas in Mexico have subsidized their families who remained in rural areas, planting unprofitable subsistence crops.[2] On a less savory level, the profundity of the crisis was somewhat ameliorated for thousands of people who are associated with the producers and traffickers of marijuana and opium poppies. Ingenuity, energy, productivity, and coop- eration have allowed extended families to stay afloat through the country's most severe economic crisis since the Great Depression and, many believe, have staved off social unrest that might have been sparked by the austerity regime.[3] The war economy strategy examined in this chapter proposes to tap into this creative and productive potential and, with proper incentives, redirect these forces, channeling them into efforts to solve the crisis in a collective mobilization to rebuild the economy. The war economy strategy would strengthen the internal market by boosting purchasing power and by simultaneously supplying food items and light consumer goods that Mexicans need to improve their living standards.

For the first time in more than a decade, there now appears to be a widespread realization among working people not only that the crisis is severe, but also that the solution is in their collective hands. The tepid opposition to the austerity program from the independent union movement is amply surpassed by the broad-based cynicism among virtually all sectors of the population. This popular defiance found its most vivid expression in the substantial erosion of support for the ruling party (the PRI) during the 1988 presidential elections, which were won only by resorting to widespread fraud; this lack of support was even more evident in the 1989 state elections when apathy, fear, and fraud combined to allow the government to impose its will and limit opposition party gains even where the PRI admitted its defeat.

The awareness of a need for broad-based solutions has even spread from the people to become part of some official analyses of the current situation. Within the ranks of the ruling party, many leaders have begun to encourage study groups to rekindle the debates of yore about alternative development approaches, if only as food for thought rather than manna for the masses. For the proposed strategy to be adopted, the government must recognize the limitations of its current strategy of debt renegotiation and export promotion. Policy makers and Mexican citizens alike must also be convinced that the country can overcome the present crisis by using their skills and resources to produce the goods required by the majority of Mexicans. This new consciousness must then be transformed into a social mobilization. In Mexico, the state itself must join with other social groups to forge a unified campaign to implement the strategy. The challenge at hand is to unleash the collective energies of the people for the task of reconstruction, based on a model that offers tangible improvements in living standards in the short term.

The war economy strategy combines administrative measures to reorient and stimulate production with market mechanisms to transmit information to the producers so they will take the initiative to promote further increases in production. This mixture of techniques is based on the supposition that a command approach (based on central planning) is neither desirable nor effective in achieving structural change in Mexico. The proposed strategy is attractive because it promises to increase employment and raise living standards rapidly by stimulating the production of basic consumer goods. It would also generate economic recovery by displacing food imports, stimulating agro-exports, and generating additional demands for manufactured goods from industries with substantially underutilized productive capacity. As an added benefit, it would even lead to a reduction in the government's budget deficit. Once the fundamental structural changes have been implemented, the market would be better able to allocate resources effectively to promote future growth. The rest of this chapter provides details of how the program would be implemented and its anticipated impact on Mexican society.

The Proposal and Its Direct Effects

The new approach has two interrelated facets. First, by raising grain prices substantially, it would be possible to assure a dramatic increase in basic grain production by mobilizing reserves of under- and unused productive capacity presently available in Mexico. This would immediately revive the rural economy by increasing the incomes of small farmers and rural day-laborers.[4] Second, an official decree to double the 1990 minimum wage, to restore consumers' purchasing power of 1980, would raise all wages in the urban economy (the increase would have to be regularly revised to preserve the new, higher level). Urban workers would be the primary beneficiaries of this feature of the program, which would end the wage repression policy, a key part of the stabilization programs of the 1980s. Together, these two propositions would create millions of new jobs and redistribute income so as to stimulate the domestic market and induce a process of demand-driven economic growth. Due to Mexico's abundant resource endowment, these two policy packages do not require any significant modifications in the export-based agricultural and industrial development and labor-intensive manufacturing assembly schemes that form the cornerstone package of present policy.[5]

The new urban wage policy would have several important salutary effects. In addition to the obvious political benefit of actively garnering the support of the urban labor force for the program, the new wage levels would strengthen and consolidate a severely eroded domestic market. Higher wages will reverse the recent deterioration in the standard of living suffered by most Mexicans, bringing real wages back to 1980 levels. As we shall see shortly, this rise in wages would also benefit *all other* groups in society and would reduce the government deficit, by raising tax revenues even more than the cost of higher wages to public employees. The new policy would also end subsidies on tortillas, generating an important savings to the government and further reducing the federal deficit.

However, the wage policy must be accompanied by a rural development strategy based on a substantial increase in the real price of basic grains, to achieve the high levels of growth and broad distribution of income required to overcome the crisis. The new price level would offer small farmers working in average conditions in rainfed areas a stimulus to increase production by guaranteeing them a payment equal to the minimum salary for every day devoted to cultivation of basic grains. Complementary measures necessary to increase productivity in rainfed areas include a direct system of credit for basic grain production, the timely distribution of fertilizers, chemical treatment of seeds to raise their germination levels, and technical assistance. These measures would allow the country to replace present grain imports with domestic production.[6]

Inflation

The proposal to raise grain prices and urban wages will undoubtedly exert an upward pressure on prices throughout the whole economy. The impact of the rise in food prices on the cost of living will be relatively small for all but the poorest families, as grains are a fraction of their total household budget; for middle- and upper-income groups, the change will be imperceptible because of the small share of basic agricultural prices in their total consumption budget. A program of food aid for the neediest would be much less costly than the across-the-board subsidies presently used to keep grain prices low. The proposal to restore the purchasing power of urban workers' salaries will have a more significant bearing on domestic price levels.

The inflationary effect of these measures, however, should be limited by the nature of the adjustment program. Since there is substantial underutilized productive capacity in precisely those areas of the economy where demand will increase, the program will prompt an immediate mobilization of existing installed productive capacity. Thus, the existing plants and equipment can be used more intensively and worker productivity will rise substantially, as generally happens in periods of economic recovery. Furthermore, it is reasonable to expect that worker productivity will rise and turnover fall as a result of higher wages.

During recent years the government has used its powers of moral suasion to convince different economic groups to subordinate their own economic interests to those of the nation as a whole. The succession of *pactos* imposed during the 1987–1990 period is testimony to the government's considerable ability to extract such commitments in the name of national solidarity. The war economy program would require a further test of this ability, but with the significant difference that it offers to reverse the deterioration of income that the majority of Mexicans have suffered during the 1980s while also channeling important benefits to those industrialists and merchants who have not enjoyed the benefits of export promotion schemes. Thus, in addition to cutting costs by increasing productivity of both labor and capital, the war economy strategy would restrain price increases by offering the promise of national economic recovery as a justification for producers and merchants to reduce their profit margins even further. As will become clear later in this chapter, producers and merchants, along with the majority of

Mexicans, would receive higher absolute incomes because of the greater volume of production and sales.

The reduction of the government deficit and the increased availability of foreign exchange would help reduce inflationary pressures. By stimulating economic growth, the war economy would increase government revenues even more than government expenditures for higher wages. Furthermore, the elimination of expensive subsidies for basic foodstuffs and for the operation of the irrigation districts would also decrease the need for the government to resort to deficit financing, while still providing an ample margin to implement an efficient food aid program for the neediest groups in Mexican society. Exports would rise as farmers in the irrigation districts switch from grains to more suitable fruit and vegetable products and food imports would decline as a result of greater domestic production.

The war economy strategy would require an adjustment period during which prices would continue to be strictly controlled. It would be essential to guarantee that urban wages and basic grain prices continue to be adjusted to maintain their new, higher real values, to the extent that other prices in the economy rise. This aspect of the program is crucial because economic recovery under the war economy strategy depends on raising the living standards of most Mexicans who have endured the worst effects of the austerity programs. The model of reconciliation implicit in the war economy model offers an attractive reward to all sectors of Mexican society in return for redressing the profound social and economic imbalances that emerged as a result of the unfortunate policies of past years (Barkin and Esteva 1986). Such a reconciliation process would facilitate collective efforts to contain inflationary pressures by reducing the social tensions occasioned by austerity.[7] In this new political milieu, any inflationary impact would be more readily accepted by the population as the cost for economic reconstruction.

Production

The Mexican war economy strategy would promote important changes in production. The volume of grain harvested in rainfed areas would multiply. Higher prices and improved profitability of maize and other basic grains would induce farmers to prepare and cultivate their lands more intensively, by using or increasing the doses of fertilizers. Presently unused areas would also be returned to cultivation, while others would probably be prepared for future use, should the farmers become convinced that the priority accorded to grains is not simply a passing fancy. The resulting increase in the harvest of maize and other basic food crops would displace the growing volume of imports, with corresponding savings in foreign exchange.

The new program would also stimulate agricultural production for export by encouraging farmers with irrigated lands to cease cultivating grains. By raising user fees in irrigated areas, the program would make the operation and maintenance of water storage and distribution systems in agriculture self-financing. Were the present water subsidies eliminated, farmers would be obliged to search for more intensive and effective ways to use water; once water became a significant cost in farming, a higher price for grains would not offset the increased cost of irrigation water.

As producers with irrigated lands begin to search for new crops to plant, exportable products are likely to be the most attractive. Domestic credit and marketing channels are inadequate for facilitating this transformation, but outsiders are anxious to make substantial investments. U.S. agribusiness has shown a growing interest in expanding production into Mexico because of rising costs for land, labor, and water and because of environmental restrictions in their traditional planting areas. The Mexican government has already paved the way for expanding foreign participation by broadening the definition of labor-intensive manufacturing assembly operations to include foreign investment in agriculture. Wealthier Mexican farmers with access to water and credit would substitute profitable export crops for grains as a result of the higher costs of production due to the elimination of water subsidies; many would have to seek out joint ventures with foreign growers and brokers to finance their efforts.

The stimulus to agricultural production—raising the price of basic grains and eliminating the water subsidy to encourage agro-export production—would generate a dramatic increase in rural employment. Although grain cultivation is not the most labor intensive of agricultural activities, the changes contemplated under the war economy strategy would create millions of new jobs. In rainfed areas, maize production presently requires about 30 person-days per hectare to produce an average of slightly more than 1.5 tons. To replace current annual imports of 4–5 million tons of maize and supply growing internal needs would require bringing into production about 3 million hectares of idle land and/or intensifying the cultivation of a larger area already under production. Mexico has abundant land already in the hands of small producers with which to reach this goal. The labor needed for the maize crop would be the equivalent of at least 400,000 additional workers, although at harvest season a greater number of farm hands would be required. The labor requirements per hectare in areas sown with wheat and sorghum are substantially lower because the harvests are predominantly mechanized, but the addition of several million hectares of rainfed land sown with these crops would create significant demands for new farm hands.

With the change from grains to agro-export crops in the irrigation districts, hundreds of thousands of additional jobs would be generated. Fruit and vegetable production requires considerably more labor per hectare than grains. Thus, the switch to intensive truck farming—which is less subject to mechanization and requires more agrochemical applications than grains—would require large numbers of new workers in the rural labor force. This would be the case even if truck farming occupied only a small fraction of the lands presently producing grains. The change would also lead to more employment in rainfed agriculture, as cultivation expanded to replace the grains produced on irrigated lands.

Thus, the war economy strategy would frontally attack Mexico's current major economic problems. It would generate more than 1 million new jobs in agriculture while raising wages and living standards for every group in society. Food imports would be largely eliminated and agro-exports increased, while the present industrial export and labor-intensive manufacturing assembly programs would remain unaffected. In the rest of this chapter, I shall examine some of the steps required to implement the program as well as discuss its impact on the society.

The Implementation of a New Policy

In the present environment, for a new economic program to be successful it must be readily understood by the populace and easily implemented. The Mexican war economy program meets these criteria. The point of departure for such a program would be an official recognition of the need for a popular mobilization to overcome the crisis. A presidential call for solidarity to support such a program is possible in the present political environment. It would, in and of itself, galvanize Mexican society, which is now in desperate need of decisive leadership. As will be evident in the subsequent analysis, the powerful urban industrialist and merchant classes also benefit substantially from the increase in well-being of urban workers and small rural farmers, as the initial stimuli increases production and sales throughout the economy.

The wage and price increases for basic agricultural products could easily be implemented through existing institutional channels, such as the National Minimum Wage Commission or CONASUPO (Compañía Nacional de Subsistencias Populares, or National Basic Goods Company, the price regulating and food distribution organization). One important modification would be ending subsidies for urban consumers of agricultural products; thus, a rise in the price of grains would be immediately translated into an increase in the price of tortillas and other grain derivatives. The resulting price increases would have a small impact on the cost of living because grains are only a small part of family expenditures. These price increases could be readily absorbed by most people, who would receive a proportionately greater increase in wages. Because the proposed program will reduce the number of households in poverty from more than 50 percent to about 37 percent, as mentioned in the last section of this chapter, such price increases can easily be justified as part of the cost of a broad-based program for economic recovery.

The mission of the Secretary of Agriculture and other official rural support agencies would be modified. In the new scheme, the focus of these agencies would change from a primary emphasis on providing institutional support and technical assistance to farmers with irrigated lands to working with small farmers in rainfed areas. The few personnel and scant resources of the extension services would offer a new source of support for this historically neglected group in Mexican society. Distribution and administration of credit would be organized directly by the farming communities themselves rather than through the cumbersome bureaucracies. Recent experiments with programs like the "credit secured by good faith (*crédito a la palabra*)" program attest to the viability of this approach. Throughout the sector, there is substantial room for trimming official expenditures in these agencies and programs and thereby achieving budgetary savings.

In sum, the implementation strategy would involve a contraction of the state apparatus required to administer the economy. Existing agencies would continue to implement their various programs, but many important functions, such as the maintenance and operation of the irrigation districts and the supervision of credit, could be transferred to the farmers.

The Rural Response

The experience of the ambitious but short-lived Sistema Alimentario Mexicano (SAM) program from 1980 to 1982 illustrates the responsiveness of farmers on rainfed lands to higher prices and profitable production. The only time since 1972 when Mexico did not suffer substantial foodgrain shortages was in 1982, when basic grain prices were temporarily increased under SAM. Alarmed by burgeoning food imports and financially bolstered by high oil prices, the Mexican government initiated the SAM to stimulate basic grain production on rainfed lands. In practice, however, agricultural production policies under the SAM program were not targeted to small farmers on rainfed lands. The SAM stimulated use of fertilizer and some other inputs on small farms, but it did not significantly increase the flow of credit for productive investment in rainfed agriculture or support the development of new technologies suited to rainfed farming. Credit policies and research continued to favor commercial farms, especially on irrigated lands in northwestern Mexico. Across-the-board increases in purchase prices for basic grains, however, had the effect of lessening the traditional bias against small producers, stimulating production of marketed foodgrains from rainfed lands.[8] As a result, maize imports as a share of total CONASUPO supply dropped to 3 percent in 1982, compared to an average of more than 50 percent since 1982. President Miguel de la Madrid abruptly dismantled SAM in 1982 following a sharp drop in world oil prices. But a major lesson of SAM remains: Even given substantial unfavorable biases in agricultural production policies, small farmers appear to respond impressively to increased prices for basic grains and to other production incentives.

The war economy strategy goes beyond the SAM experience: Like SAM, it calls for increased production incentives and support for rainfed agriculture in the form of higher official prices for marketed grains on the output side; unlike SAM, the strategy would directly improve access to credit, modern inputs, and technology to rainfed lands of smallholders to increase production and rural incomes. In this way, the war economy strategy is consistent with the spirit of SAM. At the same time, this approach avoids the inefficiencies that plagued SAM during its short lifetime. Instead of incurring huge public deficits to subsidize farm inputs, output prices would be increased, both in absolute terms and relative to other crops, to stimulate grain production. Generous input subsidies (especially for irrigation) would be removed for commercial farms on highly productive lands, encouraging a more rational and efficient use of these lands.[9]

Productivity in rainfed agriculture would also rise considerably. At present, grain production in dryland agriculture is severely restricted by low guarantee prices. Small farmers subsidize their own production, accepting wages far below those required for their sustenance and often actually injecting additional cash to pay for inputs and harvest costs. Under these circumstances, they have a substantial incentive to minimize their work and cash outlays, which severely lowers production. Because of this, crop yields per hectare have not increased measurably in more than two decades. If production were to become profitable while offering a minimum wage, maize producers would once again have a strong incentive to increase productivity. The profitability of maize production from 1940–1960 for both the market and on-farm consumption brought impressive increases in production (see Chapter 2, particularly Figure 2.1).[10] Thus, it might be expected that output costs in rainfed areas might actually decline as yields rose with more intensive use of available resources, which is what happened with wheat production in irrigated areas in the 1960s.

The Impact on Consumption

Poor consumers would be hardest hit by the price increases. Consumer price subsidies would be required to ensure that their basic food needs are met. At present, the federal government, through CONASUPO, generously subsidizes foodgrain consumption for urban consumers while providing little support for rural consumers. These nontargeted urban price subsidies offer no stimulus to producers; are of limited benefit to middle- and high-income consumers, who spend a very small proportion of their incomes on grain products; and contribute to the rapidly expanding public deficit. If only those in need were targeted, the total cost would be substantially reduced. A viable food distribution program like the existing milk program administered by LICONSA (Leche Industrializada CONSUPO, a CONASUPO subsidiary that has become a model of efficiency both domestically and internationally) could be expanded to include a basket of basic foods or a food-stamp program like that used in other countries and could be targeted directly at the most needy consumers. Such a program would be less costly than the inefficient, across-the-board subsidies for tortillas and certain other basic foodstuffs in urban areas.

Under the proposed program, CONASUPO's role in Mexican society would change. It could become more focused on its original mission of regulating the national market for basic foodstuffs. As a regulatory agency, CONASUPO would retain primary responsibility for foreign trade in grains, to assure an appropriate balance between domestic needs and total supplies. It would have sole authority to negotiate with other governments for the acquisition of grains under international programs, such as those of the Commodity Credit Corporation of the United States. It would no longer need to buy basic food products from domestic growers, because the private sector would take over this function. On the consumption side, therefore, the war economy promises to sharply reduce the cost of government programs while increasing their ability to protect the neediest groups.

Induced Effects on the Economy: The Multiplier

Some of the benefits of the Mexican war economy to small farmers and urban workers would be redistributed to other sectors of society as these two groups of primary beneficiaries spent their incomes. To trace the derived effects of these important changes, I have used two different analytical tools developed for this purpose. Both are based on the input-output table of the Mexican economy, which describes the way in which different economic sectors and social groups relate to each other. These tools identify how the initial policy changes outlined above will generate further modifications in the economy and distribute benefits among all social groups.

The easiest of the two to understand is the employment multiplier, developed originally within the Keynesian school of thought. In its application to the Mexican economy, Etelberto Ortiz Cruz (1989) shows that for every direct increase of 100 jobs in primary production (the agricultural sector), another 80 jobs will be created in the manufacturing and service sectors.[11] These 80 additional jobs would be created by the increased spending of small farmers to raise their production—for land improvements and for additional agricultural inputs for their crops—and to improve their living conditions—for food, clothing, home improvements, appliances, etc. Thus, if the agricultural program to increase basic grain production requires 1 million additional workers (the minimum increase that we might expect), at least another 800,000 jobs will be created in the rest of the economy.

The second model analyzes the spending patterns that follow from the increase in incomes that would result from implementing the war economy policies. Using a social accounting matrix, the expenditure analysis extends the input-output scheme to trace the effects of each policy option on different productive sectors, social groups, and institutions (Adelman and Taylor 1989).[12] In the following sections, I present in some detail an analysis of the impact, first, of the wage and price increases taken separately and, second, of the combination for a view of what would be the cumulative effect on the country.

The Return to Food Self-sufficiency

Raising producer prices would generate greater benefits throughout the economy than any other single policy. If the deliberate restraint of producer prices for basic grains, aggravated since 1982, were abandoned in favor of measures to stimulate basic grain production and permit the country to reach food self-sufficiency, national income (gross domestic product, or GDP) would begin to rise at a rate of 10 percent per year, the budget deficit would be 6.5 percent smaller, the trade surplus would be 47 percent larger, and personal incomes would increase significantly.[13]

With higher prices and the greater availability of resources to plant grains in rainfed agriculture, economic conditions in urban as well as rural areas would improve dramatically. Agricultural productivity could

TABLE 7.1
Economy-wide Effects of a
$1 Exogenous Increase in Small-Farmer Income

Production	Amount	Household Incomes	Amount
Basic grains	$.14	Small farmer	$1.18
Livestock	.18	Rural worker	.07
Other agriculture	.15	Urban worker	.62
Petroleum	.05	Urban marginal	.12
Fertilizer	.01	Subtotal: Labor	1.99
Ag processing	.57	Urban capitalist	.66
Industry	.85	Merchant	.32
Services	.93	Commercial farmer	.10
		Subtotal: Capital	1.08
Total Effect on		Total Effect on	
Production	$3.57	Household Incomes	$3.07

Source: Adapted from Irma Adelman and J. Edward Taylor, "Is Structural Adjustment with a Human Face Possible?: The Case of Mexico," Giannini Foundation of Agricultural Economics Working Papers No. 500, Dept. of Agricultural and Natural Resource Economics, University of California–Berkeley, February 1989.

be expected to rise rapidly, as it did during the 1940–1960 period. Increases in grain production (17 percent) would be accompanied by important improvements in other areas of agricultural and livestock production as well as in food processing and services (each would increase 6–7 percent). The enormous power of the small farmer to stimulate further economic growth in the rest of the economy is evident in the quantitative results produced by Adelman and Taylor (1989) when they used the social accounting matrix to trace the impact of the initial increase in small-farmer incomes as other people, in turn, spend the money they receive from the farmers (Table 7.1). Every additional $1 million of income received by small farmers will result in a total increase in expenditures for goods and services in Mexico of almost $3.6 million. Significantly, 69 percent of this increase would be spent in urban areas on industrial products ($.85 out of each $3.57 increase), services ($.93), and commerce ($.69). The wage hike for urban workers (analyzed in the next section), in contrast, would generate total new consumer spending of only $2.8 million.

Incomes of rural households would rise significantly: For every million pesos of additional income received by small farmers, total income of households in all sectors of society would rise by more than $3 million. Small-farmer families could expect to enjoy a real increase of 14 percent more than their incomes in 1986 and 26 percent more than what they earned in 1980. Families of rural workers and commercial farmers would receive increases of 4–5 percent over 1986 levels. Perhaps surprisingly, urban workers and informal sector groups would benefit substantially: As the rural population spent its new income on goods produced by urban and informal-sector workers, the latter's incomes would rise by 6–8 percent. Given the existing concentrated control over production and marketing, urban industrialists and merchants would continue to capture an important part of the benefits: Their incomes would rise by 14 percent and 10 percent, respectively.

At the national level, this rural strategy would produce particularly attractive results. Economic growth would have increased by an impressive 10 percent annually over that experienced during the 1980–1986 period. This strategy would also have favorable income distribution consequences for Mexico: 35 percent of the total increase in income would go to capital while 65 percent would go to labor, in contrast to the prevailing pattern that distributes 72 percent of income to capital and 28 percent to labor. The number of households earning less than the minimum wage would fall from the 1986 level of 51 percent to 43 percent. The government deficit would decline by almost 6 percent, as tax receipts increase faster than the expenditures required to support the program. The trade surplus would increase sharply (up by 46 percent) as food imports plummet and agro-exports rise gradually.[14] Thus, the proposed small-farmer development strategy tends to favor small-scale, labor-intensive industries, while contributing to improving the foreign trade account and expanding employment in Mexico. Clearly, the war economy strategy offers far more advantages as a way of promoting national development than the present policies that stimulate commercial farming at the expense of rainfed agriculture.

A Rise in Urban Wages

A reversal of the wage repression policy would benefit urban workers. These people—including professionals, government employees, industrial workers, and members of the informal sector—would spend their new incomes primarily on: (1) agricultural products, especially grains and meat, (2) processed foods, and (3) services (total demand for each would rise 6 percent). Though to a lesser degree, they would also spend more for light manufactured products, including household goods and electrical appliances (an increase in demand of 3.7 percent each).[15] However, because these expenditures by the urban workers would, in turn, improve economic prospects for other groups, the final effect of the improvement in wages for urban workers would be widely disseminated throughout the society.

Once the secondary impacts had percolated through the system, urban and informal-sector workers would enjoy a net increase in their real incomes of 8 percent and 10 percent, respectively, compared to their 1986 incomes. The remaining 75 percent of the initial wage hike boosting workers' household incomes would be redistributed throughout the marketplace. The increased demand for food products leads to important increases in real rural incomes: Small farmers would enjoy a 5 percent increase; rural wage-laborers, almost 10 percent; and large-scale farmers, 3.4 percent. In the urban areas, merchants benefit from increased sales that would raise their incomes more than 8 percent, while capitalists who produce light consumer goods reap the largest gains from the program: Their incomes would increase more than 10 percent.

Overall income (GDP) for the country as a whole would have been 8.8 percent higher without the sharp reduction in real wages than it actually was in 1986; the number of households in absolute poverty (earning less than 16,000 1980 pesos a month, which is equivalent to the minimum wage) would decline from the 1986 level of 51 percent to 38 percent.

A program to raise real urban wages would also improve the economic health of the nation as a whole. Government expenditures would rise 7 percent according to these calculations, as a result of higher wages paid to bureaucrats and public enterprise employees, but receipts from the value-added and income taxes would increase almost 15 percent, leading to a net decline in government spending of about 8.5 percent. The trade surplus would decline slightly (2.4 percent), because some of the higher incomes would be used to import consumer goods; imports would rise less rapidly than at present because the urban workers would consume fewer imported goods than do the beneficiaries of the present development model.

Thus, the single measure of restoring real wages to their 1980 levels would have dramatic positive effects on the Mexican economy. In fact, the analysis confirms "that much of the current [Mexican] economic disaster was due to a wrong policy choice" (Adelman and Taylor 1989:19). A rise in wages for urban workers would rapidly benefit every sector of the society while starting the country on the path of renewed economic growth with reduced budget deficits.

Food Supply in a Global Context

The Mexican war economy strategy is also important because it promises to return the country to food self-sufficiency. In light of the present tendency for many third world countries to increase their dependency on imported foodgrains as a result of the same forces that are operating in Mexico (Barkin, Batt, and DeWalt 1990), the move toward self-sufficiency in Mexico should be viewed not simply as desirable but rather as necessary. In 1987–1988, widespread drought combined with social forces to reduce global production below consumption, causing grain reserves to decline alarmingly and prices to rise. There are many people who now argue that the impending global warming, as a result of the "greenhouse effect," raises the specter of more frequent occurrences of drought in the coming years. When declining production is combined with increasing food dependency as countries complete their integration into the global economy and the commercialization of their agricultural sectors, it becomes clear that those countries with the ability to supply their own needs should carefully reexamine the pressures that are moving them in the opposite direction.

The decline in the capacity to achieve food self-sufficiency is not only an economic problem. In Mexico, as in most other third world countries, basic food producers frequently do not have the ability to shift from their traditional products to commercial crops for lack of access to modern inputs or the credit to obtain such inputs. Thus, if basic foodstuff production becomes unattractive, the farmers and their lands are often idled, depriving the country of its food supplies and the rural families of their means of livelihood. With the erosion of this traditional food-producing capacity, natural resources deteriorate and the social structures that supported these activities unravel. Of course, the commercialization of agriculture and the importation of basic foodstuffs also often contributes to a deterioration of diets, as modern technology threatens the variety of collateral hunting and gathering activities that are often integral to the traditional basic food–producing economy. The loss of food self-sufficiency, then, is not simply an aesthetic issue of the desirability of preserving a numerous social group, but is also a question of individual well-being, long-range national economic and social planning, and ecological balance in a world economy and society increasingly less prepared to confront the needs of poor people in poor countries.

The War Economy: An Option for Mexico?

The war economy strategy proposed in this chapter combines two policies—an increase in grain prices and a boost in urban wages—and yields final results that are more than the sum of the gains generated by each of the two policies. By reversing the wage repression policy and stimulating small-farmer production, national income would rise by more than 10.5 percent per year over what was achieved in 1986. The combined approach would improve income levels for all social groups. Not surprisingly, the small farmers would be the chief beneficiaries, reaping a 14.6 percent increase in household income over the 1986 base year levels; agricultural laborers, urban workers, and members of the informal sector would each enjoy a 9–10 percent increase. Capitalists and merchants also would continue to enjoy important benefits, receiving 12 percent and 10 percent gains in income, respectively, while commercial farmers would lag behind with only a 4 percent rise, which would increase dramatically if they were to change their cropping patterns as foreseen in the present proposal.

The combined approach also offers other benefits. The government deficit would decline more (9 percent) than with either of the two policies implemented singly, because faster economic growth would lead to rising revenues. Even before the enormous jump in food imports in 1989, the foreign trade surplus would have soared to almost 50 percent above its 1986 level of $380 billion, substantially relaxing international restraints on the economy; the improvement from 1989 levels would be even greater. Migration from rural areas to the cities would drop sharply, as employment and income opportunities improved more rapidly on the farms. The war economy strategy would also redirect future growth into those very industries, such as the light consumer goods industries and agricultural machinery and construction sectors, that have been severely affected by the austerity regime and export promotion program of recent years.

An End to the Food Crisis

Mexico's present food crisis is not simply a national problem. Food is one of the most dynamic components of the U.S. foreign trade picture, and Mexico is its third most important client. Mexico's food dependency exacerbates instability in the international economy created by the debt crisis that also afflicts most food-dependent countries. However, the question arises whether a national approach to reversing the food crisis would sow the seeds for new imbalances in the international economy.

The war economy strategy would dramatically reduce food imports and probably shift much high-quality irrigated land from grain production into the more efficient production of agro-exports. In the process, real incomes of the lowest rural income groups in Mexico would be raised substantially as the relative prices of their products increased. The multiplier effect throughout the rest of the economy would also be substantial: There would be an increase of more than three dollars ($3.57) in national production for every one-dollar increase in small-farmer incomes!

To implement such a program, important changes would be needed in Mexico. Real prices for maize would have to double to permit small farmers to earn the minimum wage for working their land. Credit and key inputs of fertilizers and seeds would have to be available for, and distributed by, small farmers; this would require giving small farmers greater autonomy in the management of their own resources and the organization of their communities. Subsidies would be readjusted and adapted to guarantee that the neediest people could buy basic foodstuffs. Current mandatory cropping schemes, accompanied by substantial subsidies for irrigation water, would have to be terminated to permit a more flexible use of affected lands.

The war economy would also dramatically alter Mexico's relations with the United States. Mexico's food import-substitution program would lead to an initial savings of several billion dollars annually. It would also eventually lead to an increase in the value of agro-exports, as production on the 50 percent of irrigated land presently dedicated to grains would be shifted gradually to rainfed areas. These changes would probably attract substantial investments by U.S. agribusiness interests, singly or jointly with Mexican farmers, which would speed the growth of fruit and vegetable exports. U.S. growers are increasingly looking to Mexico to replace domestic production and respond to increasing U.S. demand as costs for land and water increase in the United States and as labor costs may rise in the wake of U.S. immigration reform.

Employment and Production

The war economy's potential contribution to employment is also important. The direct employment effect would create the equivalent of about 1 million year-round jobs. Indirect employment effects—through a shift in basic grains production from irrigated to rainfed land, freeing irrigated land for the production of labor-intensive export crops, plus the multiplier effect on other agricultural and nonagricultural activities—could add significantly more jobs to the economy, possibly making labor a new constraint on economic growth in some areas. This would diminish pressure for people to seek employment as temporary workers in the United States. Given Mexico's present total labor force of 25–27 million people, the food import-substitution approach is the only one now being discussed that offers any chance of reorganizing the economy without sacrificing the income and employment prospects of the majority of low-income groups. Should the strategy be adopted, it is to be expected that a large number of people who might otherwise seek temporary employment in the United States as undocumented workers would find it advantageous to remain in the Mexican labor force. This would reduce or possibly reverse the "muscle drain" from rural Mexico to the United States, which in 1988 spurred more than 1 million Mexicans to apply for legalization under the Seasonal Agricultural Worker (SAW) program of the U.S. Immigration Reform and Control Act of 1986.

On the production side, the war economy results would be extensive. Among the small farmers themselves, past research suggests that, once crops became profitable again, many small farmers would be flexible in adopting productive innovations that could be expected to substantially raise yields, much as these farmers did when yields doubled during the two decades after the beginning of the land distribution in the late 1930s. The commercial agricultural sector also would prosper, as suggested in the section on production, above.

Failed Austerity

In the 1980s, the farm crisis is part of a much larger and more challenging picture. Mexico's economic crisis has triggered an austerity program that has brought on a deep recession, depressed real incomes, and impoverished most Mexicans. Going beyond the IMF stabilization model, the austerity program has combined wage repression, export promotion, fiscal restraint, and steep currency devaluation. Since February 1982, when the SAM program was aborted, these measures have been coupled with the return to a bimodal agricultural development strategy that favors wealthy farmers at the expense of small-scale producers.

With the exception of a turnaround in Mexico's commodity trade deficit, the results of the adjustment program have been disastrous. By 1986, real per capita GNP had plummeted to 10.3 percent below its 1980 level. Urban groups were particularly hard hit: The real per capita income of urban workers in the informal sector fell 20.4 percent, while that of other urban workers fell 16.4 percent. At the same time, the government deficit escalated from 3.9 percent of national income in 1980 to 9.2 percent in 1986. Inflation skyrocketed to unprecedentedly high levels; by 1986, prices were more than nineteen times the levels of 1980, an increase that averages out to 63.7 percent inflation annually over six years. By 1986, the population below the poverty level had expanded to 51 percent, a frightening total of 41 million people. Clearly, the outcome of this austerity program has been unacceptable in terms of its welfare cost.

A Brighter Future

How would the war economy strategy fit into the structural adjustment policies Mexico has followed in response to the debt crisis of the 1980s? The policy experiments examined in this chapter suggest that the war economy is not only feasible, but is also likely to be a key to successful economic adjustment that leads to higher economic growth and reduced poverty.

The simulation model suggests absolute poverty in Mexico would decline by 27 percent to 30 million people, a reduction of 11 million of those now living below the poverty line. The benefits would not be directed only into rural households: All groups in Mexico would fare better in the war economy, due to income linkages within Mexico. In the welfare economist's jargon, such a policy is "Pareto optimal," meaning that it improves everyone's welfare without harming any group. The emphasis on the small farmer is critical to successful adjustment in the macroeconomy. Even the government would be better off: The budget deficit would be 10 percent less than in 1986 and the trade surplus would be substantially higher, 46.7 percent above the observed 1986 level.

The proposal for a Mexican war economy represents a substantial improvement over present policy options, which focus on freeing or generating resources through securing debt relief and boosting international trade. The war economy strategy also is far superior to alternatives that focus just on the minimum wage. The social accounting matrix demonstrates convincingly that together these two proposals—to promote food self-sufficiency through stimulating small-farmer production in rainfed areas reinforced by a program to regain the lost purchasing power of urban salaries—offer the most viable and feasible set of policies to promote national development and initiate a new period of economic growth. The interaction between the two programs would produce the widest possible support for a major restructuring of economic policy. The Mexican war economy strategy is the key to a rapid recovery of the Mexican economy from its prolonged crisis.

Notes

1. World Bank, *World Debt Tables*, Vol 1 (analysis and commentary) (Washington, D.C.: World Bank, 1988). The comments in the text are extracted from the *IMF Survey* of 22 February 1988, pp. 53–55.

2. Ironically, the Immigration Reform and Control Act (IRCA) of 1986 temporarily facilitated this transborder flow of people by making it easier to obtain temporary visas and because the Border Patrol was instructed to reduce

its raids on employers during the application period for amnesty and for seasonal agricultural worker (SAW) visas.

3. As their survival strategy, an important group from among the wealthiest population have chosen to withdraw billions of dollars from the country in capital flight. Others are enthusiastically joining with foreign investors to produce goods for export or to service the luxury demands of the elites who are prospering during the crisis. Another small group is taking advantage of the international opening of the economy to inundate the Mexican market with cheap consumer goods from abroad, which is further threatening the viability of many domestic producers.

Within the working class, families have been obliged to creatively mobilize their collective resources into the struggle for survival: More people are working longer hours in more ingenious ways. Unfortunately, some of the literature about this process conveys a tone of celebration, describing these marginal groups as heroes, rather than analyzing the global context that is forcing them to increase the intensity of their own work while reducing their standards of living and the quality of their lives.

4. For more details on the particulars of the war economy strategy as it is applied to Mexican agriculture, see Barkin and Taylor (forthcoming).

5. Even the substantial increase in production costs occasioned by the present program need not threaten the country's international competitiveness. Mexico enjoys many resource and locational advantages that are not changed by this program. Higher wages can reasonably be expected to increase job loyalty and labor productivity even while employers are increasing their investment to further increase productivity. These factors, together with the extension of the program of "moral suasion" under the stabilization plans of 1987–1990, can be expected to counteract any depressive impact of the war economy.

6. Grain imports in 1988 were approximately 7.5 million tons, of which 2.5 to 3.5 are maize (2 to 2.5 million hectares) and 800,000 are wheat (200,000 hectares). The cultivation of grains on idle lands would require about 4 million hectares to assure the replacement of imports of sorghum, rice, and other relatively minor grain crops. In 1989, imports increased to more than 10 million tons.

7. This explanation of inflation does not ignore the monetary correlates of price increases, but instead focuses on the social and political forces that influence the changes in monetary aggregates. For an application of this approach to the Mexican experience see Barkin and Esteva (1979, 1986).

8. Admittedly, the actual impact of SAM is impossible to quantify, due to inadequate data collection and unusually favorable weather conditions during 1981, the peak year of SAM. Regarding the spectacular performance of the basic grain sector during this period, however, there can be no disagreement. Andrade and Blanc (1987) note that basic grain production from 1980–1982 was far higher than in any other three-year period in Mexico's history—including periods with similar sets of weather conditions. In the most serious effort to date to assess the production impacts and costs of SAM, these researchers also found strong indications that, even in its short lifetime, SAM was successful at stimulating basic food production on rainfed lands in small-farmer areas.

9. At present, one-half of the nation's irrigated land is sown with grains. This continues because of the huge subsidies attached to irrigation water and electricity rates for pumping. Should water and power rates be rationalized, there would be a substantial incentive for farmers to switch to more valuable and profitable crops that economized on water use. If this policy were combined with the grain policies suggested in the text, the potential for further development in rainfed areas would be even greater.

10. For an extended discussion of the potential for this kind of improvement in maize output see Felstehausen and Díaz-Cisneros (1985).

11. The employment multiplier (the eighty additional jobs) is an underestimate of the real effects of the program proposed in this chapter. It is based on primary production as a whole, including livestock, forestry, and fishing as well as agriculture. Small-scale agricultural production is substantially more labor intensive than other agricultural production and the other primary subsectors; therefore, the employment multiplier for the strategy proposed in this chapter would be substantially higher.

12. The lengthy analysis conducted by Adelman and Taylor, which is the basis for this exposition of expenditure multipliers, uses "social accounting matrices" constructed from the input-output analysis for 1980. The results are based on a series of "counterfactual experiments" in social policy making. Their policy experiments differ slightly from those proposed in this chapter, but the quantitative analysis provides a close approximation to the types of impacts that might be realized if the policy package proposed here were adopted.

13. The quantitative analysis presented in this section substantially *understates* the true impact of the strategy proposed in the text. The multiplier is based on a simple transfer of resources to small-scale farmers from commercial farmers and from field hands; it also contemplates an increase in total government spending on agriculture from 9 percent to 15 percent of the total budget. The proposed program would also stimulate commercial farming and dramatically increase the demand for rural workers, both in rainfed areas as well as in the irrigation districts.

14. These estimates of the decline in the deficit and the improvement in the foreign trade account are conservative. The war economy program would lead to higher revenues (from irrigation user fees) and lower expenditures (as a result of removing consumer subsidies for tortillas) than suggested in the Adelman-Taylor experiments.

15. These conclusions are based on an application of the 1977 survey of incomes and expenditures conducted by the statistical office of the Mexican government (INEGI, or Instituto Nacional de Estadística, Geografía, e Informática). The preliminary results from the 1983–1984 survey suggest that demand for consumer goods is even more depressed than anticipated.

References and Bibliography

Aburto, Horacio. "El Maíz: Producción, Consumo, y Política de Precios," in Carlos Montañez and Horacio Aburto, *Maíz: Política Institucional y Crisis Agrícola*. Mexico City: Centro de Investigaciones del Desarrollo Rural and Editorial Nueva Imagen, 1979, pp. 129–175.

Adelman, Irma. "Beyond Export-led Growth," *World Development*, Vol 12:9, 1984, pp. 937–949.

Adelman, Irma, and Cynthia T. Morris. *Income Distribution Policy in Developing Countries*. Stanford, CA: Stanford University Press, 1978.

Adelman, Irma, and J. Edward Taylor. "Is Structural Adjustment with a Human Face Possible?: The Case of Mexico." Giannini Foundation of Agricultural Economics Working Paper No. 500. Dept. of Agricultural and Natural Resource Economics, University of California–Berkeley, February 1989.

Alponte, José María. "La Ley Ecológica," *La Jornada* (Mexico City daily newspaper), December 11, 1987, p. 5.

Alvarado, Javier, and Adolfo Figueroa. "The Ecological Recovery of the Sea Turtles of Michoacan, Mexico." Report submitted to the U.S. Fish and Wildlife Service, Endangered Species Division, and the World Wildlife Fund, October 1988. Available from J. Woody, U.S. Fish and Wildlife Service, Box 1306, Albuquerque, NM 87103.

Andrade, Armando, and Nicole Blanc. "SAM's Costs and Impact on Production," in J. Austin and G. Esteva, eds., *Food Policy in Mexico*. Ithaca, NY: Cornell University Press, 1987, pp. 215–248.

Austin, James, and Gustavo Esteva, eds. *Food Policy in Mexico*. Ithaca, NY: Cornell University Press, 1987.

Barkin, David. "Education and Class Structure: The Dynamics of Social Control in Mexico," *Politics and Society*, Vol. 5:5, 1975, pp. 185–199.

———. "Internationalization of Capital: An Alternative Approach," in R. Chilcote, ed., *Dependency and Marxism: Toward a Resolution of the Debate*. Boulder, CO: Westview Press, 1981, pp. 156–161.

———. "El Uso de la Tierra Agrícola en México," *Problemas del Desarrollo*, Nos. 47/48, Aug. 1981–Jan. 1982, pp. 59–85.

English language editions have been cited when available. All non–Spanish language references preceded by an asterisk are also available in Spanish.

*_____. "The Impact of Agribusiness on Rural Development," in S. McNall, ed., *Current Perspectives in Social Theory*, Vol. 3. Greenwich, CT: JAI Press, 1982, pp. 1–25.

_____. "The Internationalization of Capital and the Spatial Organization of Agriculture in Mexico," in Frank Moulaert and Patricia W. Salinas, eds., *Regional Analysis and the New International Division of Labor*. Amsterdam and Boston: Kluwer-Nijhoff, 1983, pp. 97–109.

_____. "Del Bache al Cenote: Un Análisis de la Sobre y Subfacturación del Comercio Exterior y su Relación a la Teoría del Desarrollo." Paper presented to the National Congress of Economists, Mexico City, Oct. 1984.

_____. "Global Proletarianization," in S. Sanderson, ed., *The Americas in the New International Division of Labor*. New York: Holmes & Meier, 1985, pp. 26–45.

_____. "Mexico's Albatross: The United States Economy," in N. Hamilton and T. Harding, eds., *Modern Mexico: State, Economy and Social Conflict*. Beverly Hills, CA: Sage Publications, 1986, pp. 106–127.

_____. "SAM and Seeds," in J. Austin and G. Esteva, eds., *Food Policy in Mexico*. Ithaca, NY: Cornell University Press, 1987, pp. 111–132.

_____. "Fugas Internacionales de Capital, Contrabando, y el Financiamiento del Desarrollo," *Estudios Económicos*, Vol. 3:2, No. 6, 1988, pp. 205–230.

_____. "La Sobrefacturación de las Importaciones: Un Estudio Empírico," *Economía: Teoría y Práctica*, No. 14, 1990.

Barkin, David, and Gustavo Esteva. *Inflación y Democracia: El Caso de México*. Mexico City: Siglo XXI Editores, 1979 (sixth printing, 1989).

_____. *El Papel del Sector Público en la Comercialización y la Fijación de Precios de los Productos Agrícolas Básicos en México*. Mexico City: Comisión Económica para América Latina (CEPAL/MEX/1051), 1981.

*_____. "Social Conflict and Inflation in Mexico," in N. Hamilton and T. Harding, eds., *Modern Mexico: State, Economy and Social Conflict*. Beverly Hills, CA: Sage Publications, 1986, pp. 128–147.

*Barkin, David, and Timothy King. *Regional Economic Development: The River Basin Approach in Mexico*. Cambridge and New York: Cambridge University Press, 1970.

*Barkin, David, and Carlos Rozo. "L'agriculture et L'internationalisation du Capital," *Revue Tiers-Monde*, No. 88, Oct.–Dec. 1981, pp. 723–745.

Barkin, David, and Blanca Suárez. *El Fin del Principio: Las Semillas y la Seguridad Alimentaria*. Mexico City: Centro de Ecodesarrollo and Editorial Océano, 1983.

_____. *El Fin de la Autosuficiencia Alimentaria*. Mexico City: Centro de Ecodesarrollo and Editorial Océano, 1985.

_____. "The Mexican Seed Industry and Transnational Corporations," *Ceres*, Vol. 19:114, Nov.–Dec. 1986, pp. 27–31.

*Barkin, David, and J. Edward Taylor. "Agriculture to the Rescue: A Solution to Binational Problems," in L. Meyer, ed., *Neighbors in Crisis*, Boulder, CO: Westview Press, forthcoming.

Barkin, David, in collaboration with Adriana Zavala. *Desarrollo Regional y Reorganización Campesina: La Chontalpa Como Reflejo del Problema Agropecuario*

Mexicano. Mexico City: Centro de Ecodesarrollo and Editorial Nueva Imagen, 1978.

Barkin, David, Rosemary Batt, and Billie R. DeWalt. *Food Crops vs. Feed Crops: The Global Substitution of Grains in Production.* Boulder, CO: Lynne Rienner Publications, 1990.

Barnett, Richard, and Ronald Muller. *Global Reach: The Power of the Multinational Corporations.* New York: Simon & Schuster, 1974.

Barr, Terry. "The World Food Situation and Global Grain Prospects," *Science,* No. 214, 1981, pp. 1087–1095.

Behar, Moises. "Nutrition and the Future of Mankind," *World Health Organization Chronicle,* No. 30, 1976, pp. 140–143.

Beltrán, José Eduardo. *Petroleo y Desarrollo: La Política Petrolera en Tabasco, Villahermosa.* Tabasco, Villahermosa: Centro de Estudios e Investigación del Sureste, 1985.

Benería, Lourdes, and Marta Roldán. *The Crossroads of Gender and Class: Industrial Homework, Subcontracting, and Household Dynamics in Mexico City.* Chicago: University of Chicago Press, 1987.

Bhagwati, Jagdish. *Anatomy and Causes of Exchange Control Regimes.* Cambridge, MA: Ballinger Publishing Company for the National Bureau of Economic Research, 1978.

————, ed. *Illegal Transactions in International Trade.* Amsterdam: North-Holland Press, 1974.

Bortz, Jeffrey, ed. *La Estructura de Salarios en México.* Mexico City: Universidad Autónoma Metropolitana, Atzcapotzalco, 1985.

Bowles, Samuel, David Gordon, and Thomas Weisskopf. *Beyond the Wasteland: A Democratic Alternative to Economic Decline.* New York: Doubleday Anchor, 1983.

*Braverman, Harry. *Labor and Monopoly Capital.* New York: Monthly Review Press, 1974.

Byerlee, Derek, and Jim Longmire. "Comparative Advantage and Policy Incentives for Wheat Production in Rainfed and Irrigated Areas of Mexico." CIMMYT (Centro Internacional de Mejoramiento de Maíz y Trigo) Economics Program, Working Paper No. 01/86. El Bátan, México: CIMMYT, 1986.

Cardoso, Fernando Henrique. "The Consumption of Dependency Theory in the United States," *Latin American Research Review,* Vol. 2:3, 1977, pp. 7–24.

Carriles Rubio, Jorge. "Comercio Exterior México–Estados Unidos: Problemas de Comparabilidad Estadística." Working Paper No. 7, Banco de México, May 1979.

Centro de Ecodesarrollo. *Producir Para la Desnutrición?* Mexico City: Centro de Ecodesarrollo, 1988.

CESPA (Centro de Estudios de Planeación Agropecuaria). *El Desarrollo Agropecuario de México: Pasado y Perspectivas.* 13 vols. Mexico City: Secretaría de Agricultura y Recursos Hidráulicos, Subsecretaría de Planeación, 1982.

Chávez, Adolfo. *Perspectivas de la Nutrición en México.* Publicación L–50. Tlalpan, México: Instituto Nacional de la Nutrición, 1982.

Chenery, Hollis B., and Michael Bruno. "Development Alternatives in an Open Economy: The Case of Israel," *Economic Journal,* Vol. 72:1, 1962, pp. 79–103.

Chenery, Hollis B., and A. M. Strout. "Foreign Assistance and Economic Development," *American Economic Review*, Vol. 56, 1966, pp. 699–733.

Chilcote, Ronald H., ed. *Dependency and Marxism: Toward a Resolution of the Debate*. Boulder, CO: Westview Press, 1982.

Comisión Nacional de Ecología, SEDUE. *Ecología: 100 Acciones Necesarias*. Mexico City: SEDUE, January 1987.

COPLAMAR (Coordinación General del Plan Nacional de Zonas Deprimidas y Grupos Marginados). *Necesidades Esenciales en México: Vol 1. Alimentación*. Mexico City: Siglo XXI Editores, 1982.

Cordera, Rolando, and Carlos Tello. *México: La Disputa por la Nación*. Mexico City: Siglo XXI Editores, 1983.

*Couriel, Alberto. "Poverty and Underemployment in Latin America," *CEPAL Review*, No. 24, 1984, pp. 39–62.

Cuddington, John T. *Capital Flight: Estimates, Issues and Explanations*. Princeton Studies in International Finance, No. 58. Princeton, NJ: Princeton University, December 1986.

de Janvry, Alain. *The Agrarian Question and Reformism in Latin America*. Baltimore, MD: Johns Hopkins University Press, 1981.

de Murguía, Valdemar. "Capital Flight and Economic Crisis: Mexico's Postdevaluation Exiles." Research Report No. 44. Center for U.S.–Mexican Studies, University of California–San Diego, 1986.

Denman, Catalina. "La Salud de las Obreras en las Maquiladoras: El Caso de Nogales," in G. de la Peña, J. M. Durán, A. Escober, and J. García de Alba, eds., *Crisis, Conflicto y Sobrevivencia: Estudios Sobre la Sociedad Urbana en México*. Guadalajara: Centro de Investigaciones y Estudios Superiores en Antropología Social (Occidente) and University of Guadalajara, 1990.

Denslo, David, Carlos Dias, and Ward Morehouse. "Technology to Aid the Poor: Constraints to Access Resulting from Privatization—The Case of Biotechnology," in D. Denslo, C. Dias, and W. Morehouse, eds., *The International Context of Rural Poverty*. New York: Council on International and Public Affairs, 1986, pp. 103–127.

DeWalt, Billie. *Modernization in a Mexican Ejido*. Cambridge and New York: Cambridge University Press, 1979.

_____. "The Cattle Are Eating the Forest," *Bulletin of the Atomic Scientists*, Vol. 39:1, 1983, pp. 18–23.

_____. "Un Panorama de la Producción del Maíz y Sorgo en el Hemisferio Occidental," in Compton Paul and Billie R. DeWalt, eds., *Sorgo y Mijo en Sistemas de Producción en América Latina*. El Batán, México: INTSORMIL/ICRISAT/CIMMYT, 1985a.

_____. "Mexico's Second Green Revolution: Food for Feed," *Mexican Studies/Estudios Mexicanos*, Vol. 1:1, 1985b, pp. 29–60.

DeWalt, Billie R., and David Barkin. "Seeds of Change: The Effects of Hybrid Sorghum and Agricultural Modernization in Mexico," in Russell H. Bernard and Pertti J. Pelto, eds., *Technology and Social Change* (2nd edition). Prospect Heights, IL: Waveland Press, 1987.

DeWalt, Billie R., and Kathleen M. DeWalt. *Farming Systems in Pespire, Southern Honduras*. INTSORMIL Project Report #1. Lexington: University of Kentucky, 1982.

De Wulf, Luc. "Statistical Analysis of Under- and Overinvoicing of Imports," *Journal of Development Economics*, Vol. 8, 1981, pp. 303–323.

DGEA (Dirección General de Economía Agrícola), Secretaría de Agricultura y Recursos Hidráulicos. "Consumos Aparentes de Productos Pecuarios 1972–1981," *Econotecnia Agrícola*, Vol. 6:9, 1982.

————. "La Producción de Granos Básicos en México. Estudio de sus Tendencias Recientes, sus Causas, y Perspectivas," *Econotecnia Agrícola*, Vol. 7:12, 1983.

Díaz Polanco, Hector, and Laurent Guye Montalvon. *La Burgesia Agraria de México. Un caso de El Bajío*. Cuadernos del CES, Mexico City: El Colegio de México, 1977.

Director, Aaron, ed. *Defense, Controls and Inflation*. Chicago: University of Chicago Press, 1952.

Dooley, Michael P., William Helkie, Ralph Tyron, and John Underwood. "An Analysis of External Debt Positions of Eight Developing Countries Through 1990," *Journal of Development Economics*, Number 21, 1986, pp. 283–318.

Dornbusch, Rudiger. "Over- and Underinvoicing of Imports: Motives, Evidence and Macroeconomic Implications." Unpublished manuscript. Massachusetts Institute of Technology, Cambridge, MA, 1987.

Eicher, Carl, and John M. Staatz. *Agricultural Development in the Third World*. Baltimore, MD: Johns Hopkins University Press, 1984.

Ernst, Dieter, ed. *The New International Division of Labour, Technology and Underdevelopment. Consequences for the Third World*. Frankfurt, West Germany, and New York: Campus Verlag, 1980.

————, ed. "Industrial Redeployment and International Transfer of Technology: Trends and Policy Issues," *Viertel Jahres Berichte*, No. 83, Mar. 1981.

*Esteva, Gustavo. *The Struggle for Rural Mexico*. South Hadley, MA: Bergin and Garvey, 1983.

Fajnzylber, Fernando. *La Industrialización Trunca de América Latina*. Mexico City: Editorial Nueva Imagen, 1983.

*Feder, Ernst. *Strawberry Imperialism: An Inquiry into the Mechanism of Dependency in Mexico*. The Hague: Institute of Social Studies, 1977.

Felix, David, and Juana Sánchez. "Capital Flight Aspects of the Latin American Debt Crisis." Working Paper No. 106. Department of Economics, Washington University, St. Louis, MO, 1987.

*Felstehausen, Herman, and Heliodoro Díaz-Cisneros. "The Strategy of Rural Development: The Puebla Initiative," *Human Organization*, Vol. 44:5, 1985, pp. 285–292.

Fernández-Kelly, María Patricia. *For We Are Sold: I and My People–Women and Industry in Mexico's Frontier*. Albany, NY: SUNY Press, 1983.

Fernández-Kelly, María Patricia, and Lorraine Grey. *The Global Assembly Line*. Wayne, NJ: New Day Films, 1986.

Fox, Jonathan. *The Political Economy of Reform in Mexico: The Case of the Mexican Food System*. Ph.D. Dissertation. Political Science, Massachusetts Institute of Technology, Cambridge, MA, 1986.

144   *References and Bibliography*

Frank, Andre Gunder. *Crisis in the World Economy.* New York: Holmes & Meier, 1980.

*Fröbel, Folker, Jurgen Heinrichs, and Otto Kreye. *The New International Division of Labour.* Cambridge and New York: Cambridge University Press, 1979.

Garreau, Gerard. *El Negocio de los Alimentos: Las Multinacionales de la Desnutrición.* Mexico City: Editorial Nueva Imagen, 1980.

George, Susan. *How the Other Half Dies: The Real Reasons for World Hunger.* Montclair, NJ: Allanheld, Osmun, 1977.

Gregory, Peter. *The Myth of Market Failure: Employment and the Labor Market in Mexico.* A World Bank Research Publication. Baltimore, MD: Johns Hopkins University Press, 1986.

Grubel, Herbert, and Peter Lloyd, eds. *Intra-Industry Trade.* London: Macmillan, 1975.

Gulati, Sunil K. "A Note on Trade Misinovicing," in D. Lessard and J. Williamson, eds., *Capital Flight and Third World Debt.* Washington, DC: Institute for International Economics, 1987.

Halhead, Vanessa. *The Forests of Mexico: The Resource and the Politics of Utilization.* Master's Thesis. University of Edinburgh, 1984.

Hardy, Chandra. "Mexico's Development Strategy for the 1980s," *World Development,* Vol. 10:10, 1982, pp. 501–512.

Hechscher, Eli. "The Effect of Foreign Trade on the Distribution of Income," in H. S. Ellis and L. A. Metzler, eds., *Readings in the Theory of International Trade.* Philadelphia: Blakiston, 1949, pp. 272–300.

Heilleiner, Gerald K. "Transnational Corporations and Trade Structure: The Role of Intra-firm Trade," in H. Giersch, ed., *On the Economics of Intra-Industry Trade.* Tübingen: JCB Mohr, 1979, pp. 159–181.

Hernández Laos, Enrique. *Productividad y Desarrollo Industrial.* Mexico City: Fondo de Cultura Económica, 1983.

*Hewitt de Alcántara, Cynthia. *Modernizing Mexican Agriculture: Socioeconomic Implications of Technological Changes, 1940-1970.* Geneva: United Nations Research Institute for Social Development, 1976.

Hymer, Stephen. *The Multinational Corporation.* Cambridge and New York: Cambridge University Press, 1980.

JEC (Joint Economic Committee of the U.S. Congress). "The Impact of the Latin American Debt Crisis on the U.S. Economy." Washington, DC: Government Printing Office, May 10, 1986.

Jenkins, Rhys. "Divisions over the International Division of Labor," *Capital and Class,* Vol. 22, 1984, pp. 22–57.

_____. *Transnational Corporations and the Latin American Automobile Industry.* Boulder, CO: Westview Press, 1986.

Jennings, Bruce H. *Foundations of International Agricultural Research.* Boulder, CO: Westview Press, 1988.

Johnston, Bruce, and William Clark. *Redesigning Rural Development.* Baltimore, MD: Johns Hopkins University Press, 1986.

Khan, M., and N. Ul Haque. "Foreign Borrowing and Capital Flight: A Formal Analysis," *International Monetary Fund Staff Papers,* Vol 32:4, 1985, pp. 606–628.

Kopits, George F. "Taxation and Multinational Firm Behavior: A Critical Survey," *International Monetary Fund Staff Papers*, Vol. 23:3, 1976, pp. 624–673.

*Lange, Oscar. *On the Economic Theory of Socialism*. New York: McGraw-Hill, 1938.

Lifschitz, Edgardo. *El Complejo Automotor en América Latina*. Mexico City: Universidad Autónoma Metropolitana, Atzapotzalco, 1984.

Linder, Stephan B. *Trade and Trade Policy for Development*. London: Allen & Unwin, 1967.

Livas, Raúl, and Bernardo Miranda Mérida. "Niveles de Ingreso y Alimentación en México: Situación Actual y Perspectivas," *Comercio Exterior*, Vol. 38:9, 1988, pp. 830–839.

Luiselli Fernández, Cassio. *The Route to Food Self-sufficiency in Mexico: Interactions with the U.S. Food System*. Monograph No. 17. Center for U.S.–Mexican Studies, University of California–San Diego, 1986.

Lustig, Nora. *Distribución del Ingreso y Crecimiento en México*. Mexico City: El Colegio de México, 1981.

———. "Crisis Económica y Niveles de Vida en México: 1982–1985," *Estudios Económicos* (El Colegio de México), Vol. 2:2, 1987, pp. 227–249.

*Luxemburg, Rosa. *The Accumulation of Capital*. New York: Monthly Review Press, 1968.

Maccoby, Michael. *The Gamesman*. New York: Simon & Schuster, 1976.

McDonald, Donogh C. "Trade Data Discrepancies and the Incentive to Smuggle," *International Monetary Fund Staff Papers*, Vol. 32:4, 1985, pp. 668–692.

Marglin, Steve. "What Do Bosses Do? The Origin and Function of Hierarchy in Capitalist Production," *Review of Radical Political Economics*, Vol. 6:3, 1974, pp. 60–112.

Meade, James M. *Planning and the Price Mechanism*. London: Allen & Unwin, 1948.

Meissner, Frank. "The Mexican Food System (SAM): A Strategy for Sowing Petroleum." *Food Policy*, Vol. 6, 1981, pp. 219–230.

Menéndez, Eduardo. "Problemática de la Salud Urbana,"in G. de la Peña, J. M. Durán, A. Escober, and J. García de Alba, eds., *Crisis, Conflicto y Sobrevivencia: Estudios Sobre la Sociedad Urbana en México*. Guadalajara: Centro de Investigaciones y Estudios Superiores en Antropología Social (Occidente) and University of Guadalajara, 1990.

Minian, Isaac, ed. *Transnacionalización y Periferia Semindustrializada*. Mexico City: Libros del CIDE, 1983.

*Moore Lappé, Francis, and Joseph Collins. *Food First: Beyond the Myth of Scarcity*. New York: Houghton Mifflin, 1977.

Morgan, Dan. *Merchants of Grain*. New York: Viking, 1979.

Mumme, Steven, C. Richard Bath, and Valerie J. Assetto. "Political Development and Environmental Policy in Mexico," *Latin American Research Review*, Vol 23:1, 1988, pp. 7–34.

Myrdal, Gunnar. *Rich Lands and Poor, the Road to Prosperity*. New York: Harper, 1957.

Niblo, Stephen R. *The Impact of War: Mexico and World War II*. Melbourne, Australia: La Trobe University Institute of Latin American Studies, 1988.

Noble, David. *America by Design.* New York: Alfred Knopf, 1977.

_____ . *Forces of Production: A Social History of Industrial Automation.* New York: Alfred Knopf, 1984.

Ohlin, Bertil. *Interregional and International Trade.* Cambridge, MA: Harvard University Press, 1957.

Ortiz Cruz, Etelberto. "Multiplicadores de Empleo en el Modelo de Insumo-Producto," *Economía: Teoría y Práctica,* No. 14, 1989.

*Palloix, Christian. *Les Firmes Multinationales et Le Procès d'Internationalisation.* Paris: Maspero, 1973.

*_____ . *L'internationalisation du Capital.* Paris: Maspero, 1975.

*_____ . *Procès de Production et Crise du Capitalisme.* Paris: Maspero, 1977.

Pastor, Manuel, Jr. "Capital Flight and the Latin American Debt Crisis." Paper presented to the meetings of the Latin American Studies Association, New Orleans, LA, March 1988.

Paulino, Leonardo A., and John Mellor. "The Food Situation in Developing Countries: Two Decades in Review,"*Food Policy,* Vol. 9, 1984, pp. 291–303.

Pearse, Andrew. *Seeds of Plenty, Seeds of Want.* Oxford: Oxford University Press, 1980.

Perelman, Michael. *Farming for Profit in a Hungry World: Capital and the Crisis in Agriculture.* Montclair, NJ: Allanheld, Osmun, 1979.

Pitner, John B., José Luis Lazo de la Vega, and Nicolás Sánchez Durón. *El Cultivo del Sorgo.* Mexico City: Programa Cooperativo de Agricultura de la Secretaría de Agricultura y Ganadería de México and La Fundación Rockefeller, 1954.

Portes, Alejandro, and John Walton. *Labor, Class and the International System.* New York: Academic Press, 1981.

Quinby, J. Roy. *A Triumph of Research: Sorghum in Texas.* College Station: Texas A & M University Press, 1971.

Rama, Ruth, and Fernando Rello. *Estrategias de las Agroindustrias Transnacionales y Política Alimentaria en México.* Mexico City: Facultad de Economía, UNAM, 1982.

Rama, Ruth, and Raúl Vigorito. *El Complejo de Frutas y Legumbres en México.* Mexico City: Editorial Nueva Imagen, 1979.

Ramesh, J., and Charles Weiss. *Mobilizing Technology for World Development.* New York: Praeger and Overseas Development Corporation, 1979.

Ramírez de la O, Rogelio. "Industrialización y Sustitución de Importaciones en México,"*Comercio Exterior,* Vol. 30:1, 1980, pp. 31–37.

Redclift, Michael. *Development Policymaking in Mexico: The Sistema Alimentario Mexicano.* Working Papers in U.S.–Mexican Studies, No. 24. University of California–San Diego, 1981.

_____ . "Production Programs for Small Farmers: Plan Puebla as Myth and Reality,"*Economic Development and Cultural Change,* Vol. 31:3, 1983, pp. 551–570.

Restrepo, Iván, with Susana Franco. *Naturaleza Muerta.* Mexico City: Centro de Ecodesarrollo, 1988.

Restrepo, Iván, and David Phillips. *La Basura: Consumo y Desperdicio en el Distrito Federal*. Mexico City: Centro de Ecodesarrollo and Instituto Nacional del Consumidor, 1982.

Restrepo, Iván, ed. *Las Truchas: Inversión para la Desigualdad?* Mexico City: Centro de Ecodesarrollo and Editorial Océano, 1984.

Roberts, Kenneth D. "Agrarian Structure and Labor Mobility in Rural Mexico," *Population and Development Review*, Vol. 8, 1982, pp. 299–322.

_____. "Technology Transfer in the Mexican Bajío: Seeds, Sorghum and Socioeconomic Change," in Ricardo Anzaldua and Ina Rosenthal-Urey, eds., *Regional Aspects of U.S.–Mexican Integration*. La Jolla, CA: Center for U.S.–Mexican Studies, University of California–San Diego, 1986.

Robinson, Joan. *Aspects of Development and Underdevelopment*. Cambridge and New York: Cambridge University Press, 1979.

Rockefeller Foundation. *Mexican Agricultural Program, 1956–1957: Director's Annual Report*. New York: Rockefeller Foundation, 1957.

Rodríguez, Gonzalo. "El Comportamiento de los Precios Agropecuarios," *Economía Mexicana*, CIDE, No. 1, 1979, pp. 89–119.

Rogers, Everrett. *Communication of Innovations: A Cross-cultural Approach*. Toronto: Collier-Macmillan, 1971.

*Ros, Jaime. "Mexico: From the Oil Boom to the Debt Crisis," in Laurence Whitehead and Rosemary Thorpe, eds., *The Debt Crisis in Latin America*. London: Macmillan, 1986.

Rozo, Carlos, and David Barkin. "La Producción de Alimentos en el Proceso de Internacionalización del Capital," *El Trimestre Económico*, Vol. 50:3, No. 199, 1983, pp. 1603–1626.

_____. "La Tecnología y la Acumulación," *Investigación Económica*, Vol. 44:175, 1985, pp. 191–213.

Salinas de Gortari, Carlos. *Primer Informe de Gobierno, 1989*. Mexico City: Poder Ejecutivo Federal, 1989, Anexo.

SAM (Sistema Alimentario Mexicano). *Primer Planteamiento de Metas de Consumo y Estrategia de Producción de Alimentos Básicos para 1980–1982*. Mexico City: SAM, May 5, 1980.

Sanderson, Steven. *Trade Aspects of the Internationalization of Mexican Agriculture: Consequences for Mexico's Food Crisis*. Monograph No. 10. Center for U.S.–Mexican Studies, University of California–San Diego, 1984.

_____, ed. *The Americas in the New International Division of Labor*. New York: Holmes & Meier, 1985.

Sassen-Koob, Saskia. "Recomposition and Peripheralization at the Core," *Contemporary Marxism*, No. 5, 1982, pp. 88–100.

Schultz, Theodore. *Transforming Traditional Agriculture*. New Haven, CT: Yale University Press, 1964.

SEDUE (Secretary of Urban Development and Ecology). *Ecología: Concertación de Voluntades*. Mexico City: Talleres Gráficas de la Nación, 1987.

*Servan-Schreiber, Jean-Jacques. *The American Challenge*. New York: Atheneum, 1968.

Shanin, Teodor, ed. *Late Marx and the Russian Road: Marx and "The Peripheries of Capitalism."* New York: Monthly Review Press, 1983.

Smith, Carol. "Beyond Dependency Theory: National and Regional Patterns of Underdevelopment in Guatemala," *American Ethnologist,* Vol. 5, 1980, pp. 574–617.

Spalding, Ruth. "Structural Barriers to Food Programming," *World Development,* Vol. 13:12, 1985, pp. 1249–1262.

Story, Dale. "Trade Politics in the Third World: A Case Study of the Mexican GATT Decision," *International Organization,* Vol. 36:4, 1982, pp. 767–794.

Suárez, Blanca, and David Barkin. *Porcicultura: La Producción de Traspatio—Otra Alternativa.* Mexico City: Centro de Ecodesarrollo and Editorial Océano, 1990.

Tello, Carlos. *La Política Económica en México.* Mexico City: Siglo XXI Editores, 1977.

Thomas, Clive. *Dependence and Transformation.* New York: Monthly Review Press, 1974.

Toledo, Alejandro, in collaboration with Arturo Nuñez and Hector Ferreira. *Como Destruir el Paraiso: El Desastre Ecológico del Sureste.* Mexico City: Centro de Ecodesarrollo and Editorial Océano, 1983.

Trejo Reyes, Saúl. *Industrialization and Employment Growth in Mexico: 1950–1965.* Ph.D. Dissertation. Yale University, New Haven, CT, 1971.

————. "La Concentración Industrial en México, El Tamaño Mínimo Eficiente y el Papel de las Empresas,"*Comercio Exterior,* Vol. 33:8, 1983, pp. 706–715.

UNIDO (United Nations Industrial Development Organization), Global and Conceptual Studies Branch. *Restructuring World Industry in a Period of Crisis—The Role of Innovation: An Analysis of Recent Developments in the Semiconductor Industry.* Document UNIDO/IS.285, 1981.

Valenzuela Feijóo, José. *El Capitalismo Mexicano en los Años Ochenta.* Mexico City: Editorial Era, 1986.

Veil, Erwin. "The World Current Account Discrepancy," *OECD Economic Outlook—Occasional Studies,* June 1982, pp. 46–63.

Vernon, Raymond. *The Technology Factor in International Trade.* New York: Columbia University Press for the National Bureau of Economic Research, 1970.

Vigorito, Raúl. *Transnacionalización y Desarrollo Agropecuario en América Latina.* Madrid: Ediciones Cultura Hispanica, 1984.

Walsh, John. "Mexican Agriculture: Crisis Within Crisis," *Science,* No. 219, 1983, pp. 825–826.

Walsh, Susan R. *Land Reform in Mexico: 1910–1980.* New York: Academic Press, 1984.

Walter, Ingo. "The Mechanisms of Capital Flight for Latin American Debtor Countries," in D. Lessard and J. Williamson, eds., *Capital Flight and Third World Debt.* Washington, DC: Institute for International Economics, 1987.

*Wolf, Eric. *Europe and the People Without History.* Berkeley and Los Angeles: University of California Press, 1982.

Wright, Angus. "Rethinking the Circle of Poison: The Politics of Pesticide Poisoning Among Mexican Farm Workers," *Latin American Perspectives*, Vol. 13:4, 1986, pp. 26–59.

*Yates, Paul Lamartine. *Mexico's Agricultural Dilemma*. Tucson: University of Arizona Press, 1981.

Yeats, Alexander J. "On the Accuracy of Partner Country Trade Statistics," *Oxford Bulletin of Economics and Statistics*, Vol. 40:4, 1978, pp. 341–361.

Series in Political Economy
and Economic Development in Latin America

Series Editor
Andrew Zimbalist
Smith College

Through country case studies and regional analyses this series will contribute to a deeper understanding of development issues in Latin America. Shifting political environments, increasing economic interdependence, and the difficulties with regard to debt, foreign investment, and trade policy demand novel conceptualizations of development strategies and potentials for the region. Individual volumes in this series will explore the deficiencies in conventional formulations of the Latin American development experience by examining new evidence and material. Topics will include, among others, women and development in Latin America; the impact of IMF interventions; the effects of redemocratization on development; Cubanology and Cuban political economy; Nicaraguan political economy; and individual case studies on development and debt policy in various countries in the region.

Index